D1624020

THE
Charles Dickens
MISCELLANY

THE
Charles Dickens
MISCELLANY

JEREMY CLARKE

First published 2014

The History Press
The Mill, Brimscombe Port
Stroud, Gloucestershire, GL5 2QG
www.thehistorypress.co.uk

British Library Cataloguing in Publication Data.
A catalogue record for this book is available from the British Library.

ISBN 978 0 7524 9888 1

Typesetting and origination by The History Press
Printed in Great Britain

· CONTENTS ·

· INTRODUCTION ·

DICKENS' REPUTATION AS A great novelist has gone up and down, and currently seems to stand very high. It might help to bear a few things in mind.

Dickens was active (and successful) before Queen Victoria came to the throne. He was in at the very beginning of a number of developments that were to shape the culture of the nineteenth century including the growth of literacy that led to larger audiences; the development of technology that produced cheaper publications; the invention of a mass transit system (the railway) that made far-flung places (and people) startlingly accessible; and the advent of successful photography that began to distribute the faces of the famous throughout the world. All of these changed the status of the writer forever. Dickens was a pioneer.

Dickens, and his work, has been extraordinarily popular for a very long time. He is, perhaps even more than Shakespeare, the supreme anti-elitist artist; someone who consciously and energetically set out to build a mass audience. The numbers were important to him, but so was the range. For a start, he outsold many of his 'rivals' by a considerable margin. When Thackeray (by any standards a major novelist) published *Vanity Fair* (by any standards a major novel), he saw himself as 'having a great fight … with Dickens' for the public's favour. He was no doubt pleased with selling 5,000 copies a month of each instalment. *Dombey and Son* sold 34,000 per month at the same time. When Dickens' first novel, *The Pickwick Papers*, appeared as illustrated monthly parts in the late 1830s, a contemporary noted:

> needy admirers flattened their noses against the booksellers' windows eager to secure a good look at the etching and to peruse every line of the letterpress that might be exposed to view, frequently reading it aloud to applauding bystanders.

People either clubbed together to buy a copy or they hired each part from a circulating library; those who could not read, listened. R. Altick's book *The English*

Common Reader (1957), about the history of reading, uses, as an example, 'the [illiterate] old charwoman who never missed a subscription tea … at a snuff shop over which she lodged when the landlord read the newest number of *Dombey and Son* to his assembled guests'. The critic Theodore Watts-Dunton used to tell a famous story of a Covent Garden barrow girl, who, when told that the great author had died, exclaimed in dismay, 'Dickens dead? Then will Father Christmas die too?'

The odd thing, then, is that Dickens is so odd. We tend to think of him as the representative great Victorian novelist, but really he made his own mainstream of one. Later writers followed his publishing innovations where they did not, or could not, follow his art. Forget for a moment that Dickens is setting some kind of standard, and he seems wonderfully strange. Miss Havisham (*Great Expectations*) lives her wedding day, every day, in a state of ghastly corruption; Krook (*Bleak House*) drinks so much gin he bursts into flames and covers the area with greasy flakes of soot; young Bailey (*Martin Chuzzlewit*) goes for a shave though he has not a trace of a beard; Good Mrs Brown (*Dombey and Son*) steals the young heroine's clothes and sends her out in rags; the starving runaway David (*David Copperfield*) sells his jacket to a man who grabs him by the hair, pays him in instalments of a halfpenny at a time (in between which he lies on his bed singing the *Death of Nelson*) and assaults him with the terrifying exclamation 'Oh, my lungs and liver … Oh, goroo, goroo!'; Jenny Wren (*Our Mutual Friend*) sits on the roof. 'Come up and be dead!' she says. 'Come up and be dead!'

But Dickens knew what he was doing. A driven man, certainly, and animated by a furious energy at times, but he kept a pretty cool eye on his audience, his money and his art. The books are how they are because Dickens wanted them that way. Sometimes it is tempting to ascribe those aspects of Dickens' work less to our taste today either to some force within him that he couldn't resist or to some spectacular naivety that prevented him from seeing the world as it was. But rarely has any artist been so ready to engage with life as it was lived in his time. The dying

Dickens was about 5ft 9in and slightly built. He was fond of loud clothes and flashy accessories. When he first travelled to America, the President's daughter herself observed of him: 'he wears entirely too much jewellery, very English in his appearance and not the best English.'

children, the desperate orphans, the 'fallen' women, the pantomime villains, the pure heroines and the cardboard heroes that we meet in some of his novels (along with the abundant evidence of genius) are not inescapable aberrations erupted from the author's subconscious – they are elements Dickens found vital to the whole shape of his work. This only makes him more interesting.

PART 1

LIVING

GROWING UP

· CHATHAM ·

'HERE THE MOST DURABLE of his early impressions were received,' wrote John Forster, Dickens' first biographer. How did the young Charles end up in Chatham? His father, John, was a clerk who worked for the navy and had set up home in Portsmouth with his wife Elizabeth. Here, three children were born: Fanny, Charles and Alfred, although Alfred died when he was just 6 months old.

In 1817 John Dickens was posted to the dockyard in Chatham and he took a house in Ordnance Terrace to accommodate his growing family: Letitia had been born during a brief stay in London in 1816, and Harriet (who died in childhood) and Frederick followed. Elizabeth's widowed sister Mary Allen was also part of the household. There was one move within Chatham:

to St Mary's Place in 1821, where another Alfred was born.

John and his family took a full part in the life of the community. They were friendly with neighbours and with the family of a local landlord, Mr Tribe; Charles and Fanny were frequently set up by their father on a table in the Mitre Inn to entertain the company with songs and ballads of the day. And it was in Chatham that Dickens began his education. He tells us through John Forster that he was taught to read by his mother, but he probably also attended a dame school with Fanny. It was not until 1821 and the move to St Mary's Place that the children were educated more formally. The new school was in Clover Lane, now Clover Street, and run by William Giles, son of the minister of the Baptist chapel next door to the family home.

• THE THEATRE •

Mary Allen married for a second time while the Dickens family were in Chatham. This was to a widowed doctor, Matthew Lamert, at St Mary's church in 1821. Matthew had a son, James, who was a little older than the young Charles, and who became a great influence upon this early part of Charles' life.

Most importantly, he accompanied Dickens to his
first visits to the theatre. This was the beginning of
a life-long passion. 'I tried to recollect,' he said in
1846, 'whether I had ever been in any theatre in my
life from which I had not brought away some pleasant

John Dickens in about 1820. (The Percy Fitzgerald
collection, with the permission of the Guildhall Museum)

association, however poor the theatre, and I protest … I could not remember even one.'

In fact, Dickens always had a great relish for bad theatre, and revisits Rochester in 'Dullborough Town', in *The Uncommercial Traveller*, to enjoy again the somewhat shaky productions he saw there. He does not spare the company, which is hard pressed to cover a long cast list:

> Many wondrous secrets of Nature had I come to the knowledge of in that sanctuary: of which not the least terrific were, that the witches in Macbeth bore an awful resemblance to the Thanes and other proper inhabitants of Scotland; and that the good King Duncan couldn't rest in his grave, but was constantly coming out of it and calling himself somebody else.

• MONEY •

John Dickens' job entitled him and his family to regard themselves as middle class. The law, the armed forces, finance, medicine and the machinery of government had all spawned huge bureaucracies and new professions that were filled by an ever-growing army of clerks and administrators. They strove, like John, to educate their boys to equip them for office life and sometimes their girls to make homes and ornament them with their accomplishments. But the new middle classes had little money behind them if they went wrong or couldn't support their large families in seizing the opportunities they had anticipated. Things could unravel very quickly.

John drew a good salary at the dockyard and he appears to have been without expensive vices. He certainly got through his money, though. And more. He borrowed £200 in 1819 and could not keep up the repayments. The debt had to be covered by his brother-in-law, Thomas Barrow. It is possible that an attempt to save money was behind the move to St Mary's Place in 1821.

By the time John was recalled to London in 1822 the debts were considerable. And the new post meant a drop in salary. His reaction to these difficulties (and perhaps this was characteristic) was to send Fanny to school to study music – quite an investment. Twice, in 1823, there were summonses for the non-payment of rates. Rent no doubt was also in arrears, and there must have been numerous outstanding tradesmen's accounts. Elizabeth Dickens attempted to set up a genteel school herself and even went as far as obtaining a suitable property. No pupils ever came.

This precarious existence must have shaped the adult Charles' attitude to money. Part of his appetite for work certainly derived from the promise of monetary reward and, conversely, an anxiety about security. But he remained his father's son in terms of his spending, throwing money at his houses, his clothes, travel and parties. Such were his outgoings, and the complicated nature of his obligations to his publishers, that, despite his huge success, it was not until his seventh novel emerged that he could declare himself secure and free of financial embarrassments. And his childhood family – John, Elizabeth and his surviving brothers and sisters – continued to be something of a worry long after Charles had grown up. John borrowed money in his son's name; he started to sell samples of his writing and his signature; he wrote begging letters to publishers, bankers and friends. Charles became so exasperated that he eventually banished both parents to Devon, where they lived for more than three years before returning to London in 1842.

• BLACKING •

Such was the family situation in 1823 that the young Charles had to go out to work, finding employment in a boot-blacking factory on the north bank of the Thames, near the site of the modern Charing

Cross station. Great numbers of children in early nineteenth-century England would have done similar work – and many much, much worse. But for Dickens, it was a kind of oblivion, an end to all his hopes and dreams.

At the young age of 11, Dickens went to work at Warren's Blacking Warehouse. He and his companions had to cover pots of boot polish (blacking) and paste on to them paper labels. He was paid 6s a week.

He kept this secret from almost everyone except John Forster, who revealed it in his 1872 Dickens biography. Forster himself had learnt of it in 1847, when Dickens produced what is now known as 'the autobiographical fragment', apparently intended to be only the first part of Dickens' own *Life of Dickens* – a plan abandoned when instead he put the substance of the fragment into *David Copperfield*. But, thanks to Forster's care of the original source material, we have the blacking warehouse in Dickens' own words:

It was a crazy, tumbledown old house, abutting of course on the river, and literally overrun with rats.

Its wainscotted rooms and its rotten floors and stair-case, and the old grey rats swarming down in the cellars, and the sound of their squeaking and scuffling coming up the stairs at all times, and the dirt and decay of the place, rise up visibly before me, as if I were there again. The counting-house was on the first floor, looking over the coal-barges and the river. There was a recess in it, in which I was to sit and work.

What was it about the episode that affected Dickens so profoundly? He thought his parents had given up on him (and bear in mind his elder sister had just been sent to a prestigious music school):

It is wonderful to me how I could have been so easily cast away at such an age. It is wonderful to me, that, even after my descent into the poor little drudge I had been since we came to London, no one had compassion enough on me … to suggest that something might have been spared, as certainly it might have been, to place me at any common school … No one made any sign. My father and mother were quite satisfied. They could hardly have been more so, if I had been twenty years of age, distinguished at a grammar-school, and going to Cambridge.

And he felt a kind of social extinction creeping upon him. In the fragment, he takes care to describe his working companions (especially their family connections and hence social status) before claiming:

> No words can express the secret agony of my soul as I sunk into this companionship; compared these every day associates with those of my happier childhood; and felt my early hopes of growing up to be a learned and distinguished man, crushed in my breast.

• PRISON •

On 20 February 1824 John Dickens was arrested. This was a distinct possibility for all debtors in the early nineteenth century if they were unable to persuade those to whom they owed money that the sum (or an agreed part of it) would eventually be forthcoming. To begin with, John was taken to a 'sponging house': secure accommodation designed to give those arrested a final chance to settle things with their creditors. Charles was sent here and there with messages and promises, to no effect. His father was taken to the Marshalsea prison, in Southwark. Charles met him there later, in the gaoler's lodge, and they both went up to his room, where, according to John Forster in his biography, they 'cried very much'.

At first John was on his own, but it was not long before the rest of the family joined him. Except Charles, of course, who continued with Warren's Blacking. A lodging was found for him at a children's boarding house in Camden, and thus, except for his rent which was paid for him, Charles set up on his own account, living off the 6*s* a week.

He missed everyone dreadfully and said so. Eventually another lodging was found for him near the prison, which at least eased that pain, but he remained, even in company he despised, horribly ashamed of his family circumstances. Once when he was kindly accompanied home by one of the other boys after an attack of some illness, he had to part with his companion on the doorstep of a stranger's house, pretending it was his own and not being able to get rid of him any other way.

In the end, a number of circumstances brought an opportunity for change. John Dickens declared himself insolvent, which led to his release from prison; he inherited some money, began receiving a pension from the navy and started working as a journalist. Although even these developments taken together fell some way short of relieving him of his money troubles, John felt able to dispense with the few shillings Charles was adding to the family income. It is possible that he had even become sensitive about his son's position, since there was a quarrel that led to Charles' departure. Charles himself never forgave his mother for patching up the family differences and arranging for him to go back. He never went back; he just carried the memory around with him always.

· 2 ·

TAKING OFF

Dickens got to school eventually. He spent two years going to a place called Wellington House – which he remembered with very little affection – but when he left, at 15, he was ready for work. This came through an acquaintance of the family who found Charles work as a lawyer's clerk with the firm of Ellis and Blackmore. This lasted about eighteen months, and a short term at another solicitor's office followed. But it was dull. Other careers were calling, and it seemed that the opportunities offered by journalism were the most pressing.

Charles Dickens at 18. (The Percy Fitzgerald collection, with the permission of the Guildhall Museum)

• REPORTING •

Dickens had family in the business, which helped. His father was writing occasional pieces, but he also had a maternal uncle making something of a name for himself in the field. This was John Henry Barrow, who in 1828 launched *The Mirror of Parliament*.

It was not long before Dickens was part of John Barrow's parliamentary reporting team and he was soon striking out writing for other publications, including the radical newspaper *The True Sun*. He tried, with Barrow's support, for a position on the *Morning Chronicle*. At first, nothing was available, but he was finally offered a permanent position in August 1834. The *Morning Chronicle* was a liberal paper and Dickens' job was to report on all parliamentary matters. This, of course, included elections (there were two in 1835) and political meetings – all around the country, before there was barely such a thing as a railway in the land. Deadlines were nevertheless overwhelmingly important and Dickens experienced many freezing, wet stagecoach journeys, bouncing about, writing on his knees, racing back to London to get his account in before the rival reporters on *The Times*.

• ACTING •

Dickens had nourished an appetite for performing from a very young age and went so often to the theatre during his first independent years in London that it was not long before he speculated upon the possibilities of a theatrical career. He was a huge fan of the comic actor Charles Mathews, who had become something of a phenomenon on the London stage with what he called his 'At Homes'. These were solo shows which combined the physical slickness of the quick-change artist with an extraordinary talent for mimicry and comic timing. They included Mathews' 'monopolylogues', in which he impersonated a variety of widely differing comic characters linked together by a short narrative. Dickens saw him many times, learned some of the 'At Homes' by heart and imitated the physical skills. When Dickens applied for an audition at Covent Garden in 1832, he described himself very much in the Mathews mould: 'I believed I had a strong perception of character and oddity, and a natural power of reproducing in my own person what I observed in others.' (John Forster's *The Life of Charles Dickens*)

He got the chance, with an invitation to do 'anything of Mathews' that he might choose, but he had to cancel, because of a terrible cold, and the acting career never materialised.

This was, of course, by no means the end of Dickens' involvement with the stage. Indeed, his amateur efforts – and there were two in 1833, in the Dickens family lodgings – were taken quite as seriously (at least by him) as many professional productions. Acting and performing is a theme that genuinely runs through his entire life and animates his art.

• WRITING •

Although Charles Dickens wasn't paid for his first published piece of work, 'A Dinner at Poplar Walk', he knew what it all meant. In the preface to the cheap edition of *The Pickwick Papers*, he tells us that he practically smuggled it into the magazine's offices – it was

> *Dickens' first published piece of creative work appeared in the **Monthly Magazine** in 1833. It was called 'A Dinner at Poplar Walk'. The publication had a circulation of about 600 and the young author wasn't paid.*

'dropped stealthily one evening at twilight, with fear and trembling, into a dark letter box, in a dark office, up a dark court in Fleet Street' – and its emergence in print was an occasion of some emotion: 'I walked down to Westminster Hall, and turned into it for half an hour, because my eyes were so dimmed with joy and pride, that they could not bear the street, and were not fit to be seen there.'

More pieces for the *Monthly Magazine* followed. These were comic stories, which owed a lot to the theatrical farces so common on the London stage. It was at the end of one of these pieces, published in May 1834, that he signed his name as 'Boz', the nom de plume by which he first began to establish his reputation, and indeed his brand. As 'Boz', Dickens began to collect readers.

He was given further opportunities to please them. He began to write occasional pieces for the *Morning Chronicle* in addition to his reporting. These were his 'sketches' – informal surveys of parts of London, London themes or observations of London people, held together by a conversational tone rather than a narrative: a Londoner talking to Londoners. When an evening sister paper to the *Morning Chronicle* was launched, Dickens obtained a salary to continue his writing explorations in the same vein. The new editor

> *Dickens also tried his hand at writing musical drama – The Village Coquettes was first performed in 1836. It was not a success. Later in life, when asked if he still possessed a copy, he replied: '… if I knew it was in my house and if I could not get rid of it in any other way, I would burn the wing of the house where it was.'*

was George Hogarth, who was to become Dickens' father-in-law within a few short months.

The increasing exposure brought Dickens to the attention of Harrison Ainsworth, a writer not much read today, but a real star of the literary scene at this time. Ainsworth must have admired Boz's work, because he introduced him to his own publisher, John Macrone, and very soon a collected volume of the newspaper and magazine pieces was on the cards. Somehow Macrone secured the services of George Cruikshank, the leading illustrator of the day. The resulting publication emerged in February 1836 as *Sketches by Boz*. It sold so well that a second edition was needed that year, and two more in 1837. Macrone soon started talking to Dickens about a second series, which appeared at the very end of 1836. Life was getting busy.

All this attention and opportunity won Dickens his big chance, and he grasped it eagerly. As the first

edition of *Sketches by Boz* emerged in 1836, he was
approached by the publishers Chapman and Hall. They
came with an idea that had been proposed to them in
turn by a well-known illustrator, Robert Seymour.
The plan went like this: Seymour would produce a
series of engravings depicting the amusing mishaps
attending a club of Cockney sportsmen; men from
the new middle classes, with money to spend on the
aristocratic pursuits of previous generations: hunting, shooting and fishing. These illustrations would be
published as a monthly serial. Would Dickens care to
write some text to help string the images together?
Fourteen pounds a month might be possible.

No one really knows, of course, what – or how
much – Dickens saw in this offer at the time. He liked
the money. We also know he was told that serials were
a 'low, cheap form of publication' that would ruin
him, and the fact that he kept all his other irons in the
fire would suggest that he didn't count too much on
the new venture establishing his reputation. But that is
exactly what it did. He claims, in the preface to what
became *The Pickwick Papers*, that he recognised from
the beginning that the idea wouldn't do:

Ivorex plaque of Mr Pickwick. Ivorex was the trade name and brainchild of Arthur Osborne, whose business in Faversham, Kent, turned out hundreds of hand-painted plaster souvenirs and ornaments over many years. (With the permission of the Guildhall Museum)

> I objected, on consideration, that although born and
> partly bred in the country I was no great sportsman
> … that the idea was not novel, and had already been
> much used; that it would be infinitely better for the
> plates to arise naturally out of the text; and that I
> should like to take my own way …

Seymour's reaction to Dickens' own plans is less than
clear, because having illustrated the first number and
got partway through the second, he shot himself in
his garden in Islington. This sent Chapman and Hall
out hunting for a new artist, but it also meant that
Dickens was now the undisputed master of the whole
project. His text was increased in length, the images
were reduced to two per month and gradually the
work began to take shape as a narrative rather than
a series of sketches. At first sales were disappointing, but by the end of its run, in November 1837, *The
Pickwick Papers* was selling 40,000 copies per month, it
had been adapted for the stage many times over and
the words of its characters seemed to be on everyone's lips – as was the name of its young author.

3

SETTLING DOWN

· DICKENS IN LOVE ·

SOMETIME BEFORE 1830, DICKENS fell in love with a young woman called Maria Beadnell, the daughter of a banker. The relationship between them flashed on and off for around four years, despite hostility from her parents, interference from friends and Maria's own capricious nature. The letters that survive show how thoroughly Dickens was absorbed in pursuing her. When the end finally came, he wrote to her, claiming: 'I have never loved and I can never love any human creature breathing but yourself.'

Many years later, he got a letter from her out of the blue and a short correspondence between them began in which he proclaimed the intensity of his original feelings for her. The tone of these letters soon changed after he arranged to see her and she turned out to be 'toothless, fat, old and ugly' (her words). Dickens later hinted very strongly that he based the character of Flora Finching in *Little Dorrit* on the older Maria.

THE HOGARTHS

The Beadnell business is interesting because of the marked contrast it makes with Dickens' engagement and marriage. Catherine Hogarth, the daughter of his boss at the *Evening Chronicle*, could hardly have been a more different young woman. At least Dickens looked at her in a completely different way. His letters to her are affectionate but occasionally overbearing, as if he is asserting himself to ensure that no more nonsense gets in the way of the matter in hand (his own ambition). He is particularly careful to outline the primacy of his work and its demands; his commitments at this period were extremely heavy. They married on 2 April 1836 and went for a week's honeymoon to Chalk in Kent (during which, true to form, Dickens was busy with *The Pickwick Papers*).

A feature of the newlyweds' relationship, and indeed of their household, was the presence of other Hogarths. There was Mary, Catherine's younger sister. She supported Catherine during her first pregnancy and went to stay with the couple when they moved to much larger premises in Doughty Street. Here tragedy struck. Having been out to the theatre with Charles and Catherine, Mary was taken ill in the middle of the night and died the following day. Dickens was completely taken to pieces by this unforeseen event and never forgot her. For the only time in his life he missed a deadline, cancelling the parts of *Pickwick* and *Oliver Twist* that were due the next month. In his address to his readers apologising for the hiatus he cited her as 'the chief solace of his labours'. He dreamt about her again and again in visionary terms. Perhaps most strangely of all, he wanted to be buried next to her and felt damaged when one of her brothers was laid there instead, writing in a letter: 'The desire to be buried next to her is as strong upon me now as it was five years ago; and I know … that it will never diminish … I cannot bear the thought of being excluded from her dust …'

But it was another Hogarth sister, Georgina, who turned out to be 'the best and truest friend man ever had' (words taken from Dickens' will). Eleven years younger than Catherine, Georgina was an indispensable part of the Dickens household from a very young age. She helped to look after the children as the family grew rapidly, travelled with them when they went abroad and was a companion and source of support to her sister and her famous brother-in-law. Most controversially, when Charles and Catherine separated in 1858, Georgina chose to stay with the children and moved with them and Dickens into the new household at Gad's Hill Place. Here, in Catherine's absence, she became a housekeeper and companion to her brother-in-law, enduring unpleasant rumours and gossip to do so. She managed the household accounts when Dickens was away and dealt with his correspondence, receiving visitors with him when he was at home. She was with Dickens on 8 June 1870, when he suffered the stroke that killed him.

• HEARTH & HOME •

Where did Dickens live? After their wedding, he took Catherine to the set of 'chambers' he was renting in Furnival's Inn, one of the inns of court, the traditional home of English law practice and accommodation for many non-lawyers too. As *The Pickwick Papers* started bringing in a more secure income, he set his sights on more substantial living quarters. These turned out to be at 48 Doughty Street, into which Charles and Catherine moved with their son Charley in March 1837.

> *Dickens owned several pet ravens. His favourite, Grip,*
> *had a large vocabulary. After Dickens died, its stuffed*
> *body was sold for £120.*

This was a finer place than he had known to date, as a man or boy, and he took Mary Hogarth and his brother Fred with him: there was certainly room. The house was taken on a three-year lease, costing £80 per year. Today this property is part of the Charles Dickens Museum.

In December 1839, the family moved to 1 Devonshire Terrace, a grand building that Dickens immediately set about making grander with internal additions and alterations. Here he spent more than ten years, writing into the middle part of his career, including well-known works such as *A Christmas Carol* and *David Copperfield*. He chose a study that over-looked the garden, with a French window to the outside. It was also a fine house for entertaining.

Larger still was Tavistock House, which became the Dickens' home in November 1851. This had been the house of an artist friend, Frank Stone, and Dickens clearly intended this to be something of a permanent settling down (after years of travel), as he took out a fifty-year lease on the property. As well as much writing, this house also witnessed the most elaborate of Dickens' private theatricals, including performances of *The Frozen Deep*, written for him by Wilkie Collins and involving a large cast and preparations that were, in his own words, 'of stupefying grandeur'.

Dickens acquired his final home while still living at Tavistock House. He saw Gad's Hill Place for sale during a walk in north Kent and recognised it as the very house recommended to him by his father many years earlier. The story is preserved for us in Dickens' essay 'Travelling Abroad'. The writer gives a lift to a 'very queer small boy' from Chatham, who asks to look at the house at the top of the hill in Higham. Why?

> … ever since I can recollect, my father, seeing me so fond of it, has often said to me, 'If you were to be very persevering and were to work hard, you might some day come to live in it.'

The narrator comments:

> I was rather amazed to be told this by the very queer small boy; for that house happens to be MY house, and I have reason to believe that what he said was true.

Dickens determined to buy Gad's Hill Place outright; and did so in 1856. It cost him £1,700. For a while the family used it as a holiday home, but after Dickens separated from Catherine, he seemed to see it as an opportunity to start again in the country. Almost the entire family (without Catherine obviously, but also Charley, the eldest son) moved in permanently in 1859. The lease for Tavistock House was then sold. After Dickens died, Charley bought Gad's Hill Place, but was forced to sell it shortly afterwards, in 1879. The house spent many years as a school but is now in the care of a specially constituted trust.

Ivorex plaque of Gad's Hill Place. (With the permission of the Guildhall Museum)

Gad's Hill Place came with a great deal of land, part of which was separated from the house by the Gravesend–Rochester Road. Here, in 1865, Dickens erected a Swiss chalet that had been given to him by the actor Charles Fechter. Not a home, of course, the chalet nevertheless became a pleasant retreat in the summer months and a favourite place to work. It can now be seen in the gardens of Eastgate House, Rochester.

• THE DICKENS CHILDREN •

Dickens and Catherine had ten children, nine of whom survived to adulthood.

Charley (1837–96) went to Eton and wanted to be a soldier, but Dickens lost patience with his progress at school and at 16 sent him off to a business school in Leipzig. This was not a particular success, and Charley worked for Barings Bank for a few years before travelling with a view to building up further commercial experience. Two attempts at setting up a business back in England failed, and eventually he joined his father's staff on his magazine, *All the Year Round*, succeeding Dickens as editor when he died. In the 1880s he toured the United States, giving readings and lectures about his father's work.

> **Dickens was a remarkably good hypnotist. His son Charley often saw him send people into a 'strange sleep'.**

Dickens' eldest daughter, Mamie (1838–96), lived at home with him always and never married. It is to Mamie that we owe one of the most compelling accounts of Dickens working, which she recounted in her book of reminiscences, *Charles Dickens by his Eldest Daughter* (1885). She had been ill and during her convalescence was allowed to remain in Dickens' study as he wrote:

On one of these mornings, I was lying on the sofa endeavouring to keep perfectly quiet, while my father wrote busily and rapidly at his desk, when he suddenly jumped from his chair and rushed to a mirror which hung near, and in which I could see the reflection of some extraordinary facial contortions which he was making. He returned rapidly to his desk, wrote furiously for a few moments, and then went again to the mirror. The facial pantomime was resumed, and then turning towards, but evidently not seeing, me, he began talking rapidly in a low voice.

Mary Angela Dickens, Charles Dickens' granddaughter, painted by her aunt, Kate Perugini (*née* Dickens) in about 1882. (With the permission of the Guildhall Museum)

Katey (1839–1929) was said to be like her father: lively and fun, but quick to take offence. There was considerable friction between them as she grew up and she claimed later that she hurried into her first marriage (to the artist Charles Collins) to escape the family home. Collins died in 1873, and Katey married another artist, Carlo Perugini, a year later. She was able to exercise her own considerable artistic talent over the following years and her reminiscences were in great demand as she neared the end of her long life.

Walter (1841–63) was allowed to be a soldier and began preparing for the Indian Army when hardly beyond his childhood years. He embarked for India at the age of 16, and met Charley there on his travels a few years later. But he was in debt and soon fell ill. He died before he was able to arrange a passage home.

Dickens wanted to get Frank (1844–86) into the Foreign Office but he ended up working at *All the Year Round* with Charley. In the end, Frank went to India to serve in the Bengal mounted police. He returned in 1871, lost all his money and immigrated to Canada to become a Mountie.

Alfred (1845–1912) was sent to school in Boulogne at the age of 7, along with Frank. An army career was on the cards but he failed his exams and eventually immigrated to Australia in 1865 to become a manager on a sheep farm. He stayed for forty-five years. On his return he decided to forge a new career lecturing about his father and reading from his work, and left for America to put the plan into action. Unfortunately, he fell ill and died shortly after his arrival in New York, in 1912.

After the school in Boulogne, Sydney (1847–72) joined the navy. Never good with money, he got into debt and was forced to ask his father many times to settle his accounts. Dickens did so but was furious. Sydney barely survived his father, dying at sea at the age of only 25.

Henry (1849–1933) was the most conspicuously successful of Dickens' sons. He studied law at Cambridge, winning a scholarship in his first year. He made great progress in his subsequent career, practising as a barrister and eventually becoming a judge. He was knighted in 1922. He had some involvement in the production of the first edition of Dickens' letters, and his own reminiscences of his father were published in 1928.

Dora (1850–51) died suddenly, before her first birthday, in the care of nurses while her parents were away. Dickens lost his father in the same year.

Edward (1852–1902), who was nicknamed 'Plorn', became something of a spoiled favourite.

Despite this, he was sent out to Australia to join Alfred at the age of only 16. Here a few false starts in sheep farming and other business ventures came to nothing. He even became an MP for a while, but took to gambling and ran up large debts. His brother Henry settled them, although there were still amounts outstanding when he died in 1902.

• GOOD WORKS •

What do we know of Dickens' political life? He was a man generally who looked for salvation in individual responsibility rather than corporate action. His indignation was a great weapon that he would wield on behalf of the oppressed, although some of his thinking about crime and punishment seems very harsh today. In a speech he made in 1869, he said: 'My faith in the people governing is, on the whole, infinitesimal; my faith in the People governed is, on the whole, illimitable.'

His charitable work, however, does demonstrate a certain pattern. In the first place, he was extraordinarily active. Although in financial terms his level of giving is not out of the ordinary by Victorian standards, the amount of time he devoted to charities and charitable causes was significant. Sometimes this got out of hand and Dickens would grumble: 'For a good many years I have suffered a great deal from charities, but never anything like what I suffer now,' he wrote to a friend in 1858. Both the giving and the grumbling are consistently reflected in his work as well as his life, as his particular concerns and pet hates are rehearsed and acted upon.

Quick to recognise and join the charitable work of others, he could also strike out on his own when he was personally concerned. This often involved both his professional talents and contact list. At the beginning of his career he organised and edited *The Pic-Nic Papers* in aid of the widow and children of John Macrone, who had published *Sketches by Boz*, and who had died aged only 28. Distinguished contributors included Harrison Ainsworth and the illustrators Browne and Cruikshank. The book raised £450. Many years later, Dickens also organised a fund to support the family of his old friend Douglas Jerrold by performing in a series of fundraising theatrical productions.

• SCHOOLS •

Education was always a priority amongst Dickens' public charitable activities. It was, though, something of a battleground. He hated the worthy air of much Church-sponsored teaching and was very suspicious of evangelicalism. This lay behind his ambivalent attitude to the Ragged School movement, although he was an early supporter and advocate. The ragged schools began in London in the 1830s and grew out of Sunday schools that had been made freely available to the children of working-class people (even so-called dame schools, like the one Pip attends in his village in *Great Expectations*, charged a few pence a week). Their purpose and organisation was formalised with the formation of the Ragged School Union in 1844. Dickens wrote about them in an influential letter to the *Daily News* in 1846.

As well as donating money himself, he visited ragged schools in London on behalf of his rich friend Angela Burdett Coutts and encouraged her to support them.

This is also a rare issue for Dickens in that he calls for State intervention, in the form of an annual grant, so that the schools would be allowed some kind of security. He does this repeatedly, and is still doing so in the 1850s. His magazine *Household Words* carried many articles supporting the movement and associated initiatives designed to intervene before poverty and desperation led young people to crime. One of his own essays from 1852, entitled 'A Sleep to Startle Us', describes a visit to a ragged school and its associated dormitory, where Dickens looks over bodies of men and boys asleep:

> It was an awful thing, looking round upon those one hundred and sixty-seven representatives of many thousands, to reflect that a Government, unable, with the least regard to truth, to plead ignorance of the existence of such a place, should proceed as if the sleepers never were to wake again.

• URANIA COTTAGE •

Dickens met the young heiress Angela Burdett Coutts in 1839. One of the very richest women in England, she became a great philanthropist and eventually Britain's first female peer. Dickens became her unofficial adviser in many charitable projects. One such project was the founding of Urania Cottage, in which former prostitutes and other 'fallen women' were offered a safe place to stay before reintegrating

In 1846, Dickens and banking heiress Angela Burdett Coutts began to plan a safe house or home for women rescued from prostitution or a life of crime. This became Urania Cottage, in Shepherd's Bush, and Dickens was to be heavily involved with it for the next ten years. The aim was to give women the chance of a new life in the colonies, but the emphasis was always very strongly on self-help and self-discipline.

them into society. He took a great deal of care over the administration of the place (there was a committee which took formal responsibility), interviewing prospective inmates, getting to know superintendents and dismissing women who had become disruptive.

Urania Cottage was not supposed to be a prison; on the contrary, its domestic environment was part of its reformatory impulse. There was some schooling. Each woman had a plot in the garden to cultivate. They were given clothes in cheerful colours and were not spoken to about whatever past they had decided to leave behind. There were failures, of course, but also many successes. One young woman returned from South Africa engaged and respectable. She bought Dickens an ostrich egg as a present.

4

ABROAD

· AMERICA ·

Dickens first went to America in order to write about it. He had an arrangement with his publishers set up before he left in 1842, and did some research before he went. It was certainly not a new idea and there was a market in Britain for descriptions and assessments of American society. The Reform Act of 1832, which slightly increased the franchise in Britain and which dealt with some of the most striking inequalities of the existing system, helped to create an interest in American democracy in action.

Dickens and Catherine crossed the Atlantic on the steamship *Britannia*, having arranged for the children (four of them at this stage) to be cared for at home. It was an extraordinarily rough and frightening crossing and both of them spent much of the time being ill. The ship even ran aground in Nova Scotia before eventually putting in to Boston on 22 January 1842. At first Dickens was delighted with everything, but the welcome was almost overwhelming. He was followed everywhere by crowds of people and was deluged with invitations. The press reported his appearance and manner in minute personal detail, and he and Catherine soon found they had to devote hours each day simply to shaking people's hands. Somehow Dickens also fitted in visits to prisons, asylums, factories and workhouses, ever mindful of the material he was collecting for his travel book. He wrote regularly to Forster, and both of them knew the letters would be the basis of the new publication.

The exhilaration of the Boston arrival soon waned. The sheer hard work of superstardom ground Dickens down and the hysterical response of the public put him on edge. He missed home, of course, and started to find fault with various aspects of American society. He couldn't escape the crowds. He hated spitting (the chewing of tobacco was a common habit amongst American men). But one issue more than anything helped things to turn sour. This was the law of international copyright: there wasn't one. Even in Britain itself regulation had been patchy. Dickens was used to hack writers pirating his work almost instantly, publishing versions of it in cheap editions, rewriting endings or adapting it for the stage. Things were tightened up with an act in the very year Dickens travelled to America, but at that date books could be published abroad without any infringement of copyright. Dickens understandably felt that he was being denied remuneration for his own work merely because thousands of readers obtained it overseas. No doubt he saw his American trip as an ideal opportunity to agitate for an international agreement to protect authors' rights.

His American hosts did not see it quite like that. They thought Dickens was being rude and ungrateful. Although he found a few public figures to support his ideas, the press became increasingly hostile. He was urged to mind his own business. 'You must drop that, Charlie,' sneered *The Boston Post*, 'or you will be dished; it smells of the shop – rank.'

A gruelling itinerary was planned. Periodically Dickens made an effort to refuse to accept any more invitations to public dinners. But the 'levees' continued, where he was shown to the public like some great natural curiosity. In Washington, he met the president but declined an invitation to dine at the White House. In Richmond, Virginia, he was so upset by what he saw of slavery that he turned back and headed north instead.

It wasn't all miserable. There were a blissful few days at Niagara Falls and, predictably, amateur theatricals to help Dickens let off steam. But June, and embarkation, were no doubt extremely welcome. Their returning sailing packet docked in Liverpool on the 29th of that month, and Dickens and Catherine headed for London as soon as they could. Poor Charley was so pleased to see them he had convulsions and a doctor was called. The travel book, when it came out, was called *American Notes*. More (and more satirical) material was to surface in *Martin Chuzzlewit*.

Dickens went to America for the second time to read. His tour of 1867–68 was a huge financial success and he put some effort into regaining public sympathy after the criticism of his earlier years. Despite this, he still found himself subject to intense scrutiny and vicious personal attacks. There were some ticketing problems: Dickens (and his tour manager George Dolby) found it difficult to circumvent the touts who bought up the reasonably priced tickets and sold them for a huge profit. He was often depicted as avaricious and ungrateful (picking up on an 1842 theme). He was targeted over his marriage and the separation from Catherine. On top of all this, Dickens was frequently ill, which made him less able to cope with the stress of touring and led him to cancel many engagements.

It is often said that this second American visit short-ened Dickens' life – or even that it killed him.

• FRANCE •

Dickens loved France and had a long, involved rela-tionship with it, which grew in intimacy during the course of his life. He loved its difference and its acces-sibility, and it seems to have given him the opportunity to be different himself – especially in his final years, when he was setting up an entire alternative life there with Ellen Ternan. His relationship with the coun-try really matured during the time he spent in Paris at intervals in the late 1840s and 1850s. He seemed to detect that the figure of the artist had a somewhat higher status there than in England, and this contrib-uted to him finding Paris 'the most extraordinary place in the World' (which he wrote in a letter to Count D'Orsay in 1844). The other important French location was Boulogne, where his younger sons went to school and which crops up in his essay writing as a companion retreat to Broadstairs in Kent:

But our French watering-place, when it is once got into, is a very enjoyable place. It has a varied and beautiful country around it, and many characteristic and agreeable things within it … It is more picturesque and quaint than half the innocent places which tourists, following their leader like sheep, have made impostors of.

Condette, just outside Boulogne, was the village where Dickens and Ternan lived together and it became the safe haven of his new life – close at hand, close to the chest too.

• ITALY •

Dickens lived in Italy for about a year in 1844–45. He always intended to write about the experience, and used the letters he wrote during his stay (especially those to John Forster) as source material. Dickens seems to have been aware that the market for travel guides was rather crowded and instead, in *Pictures from Italy*, he goes for a more opinionated piece of extended travel journalism, rather like his *American Notes*. These opinions attracted some criticism when the book was published in 1846, as, although Dickens generally steers clear of the complicated political situation at the time, his anti-Catholic feelings are very evident. Indeed, his friend Clarkson Stanfield, who had been chosen to illustrate the work (and who later became a Roman Catholic), turned down the commission once he read the material.

5

SECURITY & SECRETS

• SEPARATION •

'Poor Catherine and I are not made for each other, and there is no help for it.' This was to John Forster in 1857. Things had probably been brought to a head (at least as far as Dickens was concerned) by his involvement with, and attraction to, the daughters of the Ternan family. Frances Ternan and her two younger daughters, Maria and Ellen (known always to Dickens as 'Nelly'), had been engaged to act in Wilkie Collins' drama *The Frozen Deep*. They were needed because, although this play had begun its life in Dickens' own house as one of his 'stupendous' private theatricals, it had been taken on to the public stage to raise money for the family of Douglas Jerrold, who had recently died. And not just any public stage, but that in the

Free Trade Hall in Manchester, which could seat up to 4,000 people. This required professionals and the Ternans fitted the bill. Dickens' life changed.

He did what he could to put Catherine away from him. He moved into the spare bedroom (actually his dressing room) and sealed up the connecting door. He wrote to Angela Burdett Coutts saying that the marriage had been miserable for 'years and years'. Negotiations for a separation and a settlement were begun in 1858, by which time gossip and rumour had done their worst.

Once the separation had become an established fact, Dickens made everything much worse and certainly more painful for everyone else involved by two rash actions. He wrote a personal statement and wanted to get it published. This was an attempt at a kind of damage limitation and a way he could convince himself that he was imposing his own version of events on his public. The problem was that for the vast majority of his readership, its details (such as they were) would have been baffling, and for those in the know, it was unconvincing. *The Times* printed it in full, and Dickens himself put it in *Household Words*; but when he attempted to insist on its going into *Punch* too, understandably the publishers refused. Since they (Bradbury and Evans) also published Dickens, this was

TAVISTOCK HOUSE THEATRE.

UNDER THE MANAGEMENT OF MR. CHARLES DICKENS.

On Twelfth Night, Tuesday, January 6th, 1857, at a Quarter before 8 o'Clock, will be presented

AN ENTIRELY NEW
ROMANTIC DRAMA, IN THREE ACTS, BY MR. WILKIE COLLINS,

CALLED

THE FROZEN DEEP.

The Machinery and Properties, by Mr. Ireland, of the Theatre Royal, Adelphi. The Dresses by Messrs. Nathan, of Titchbourne Street, Haymarket. Perruquier, Mr. Wilson, of the Strand.

THE PROLOGUE WILL BE DELIVERED BY MR. JOHN FORSTER.

CAPTAIN EBSWORTH, *of The Sea Mew*	MR. EDWARD PIGOTT.
CAPTAIN HELDING, *of The Wanderer*	MR. ALFRED DICKENS.
LIEUTENANT CRAYFORD	MR. MARK LEMON.
FRANK ALDERSLEY	MR. WILKIE COLLINS.
RICHARD WARDOUR	MR. CHARLES DICKENS.
LIEUTENANT STEVENTON	MR. YOUNG CHARLES.
JOHN WANT, *Ship's Cook*	MR. AUGUSTUS EGG, A.R.A.
BATESON } *Two of The Sea Mew's People*	{ MR. EDWARD HOGARTH.
DARKER }	{ MR. FREDERICK EVANS.

(OFFICERS AND CREWS OF THE SEA MEW AND WANDERER.)

MRS. STEVENTON	MISS HELEN.
ROSE EBSWORTH	MISS KATE.
LUCY CRAYFORD	MISS HOGARTH.
CLARA BURNHAM	MISS MARY.
NURSE ESTHER	MRS. WILLS.
MAID	MISS MARTHA.

THE SCENERY AND SCENIC EFFECTS OF THE FIRST ACT, BY MR. TELBIN.
THE SCENERY AND SCENIC EFFECTS OF THE SECOND AND THIRD ACTS, BY Mr. STANFIELD, R.A.
ASSISTED BY MR. DANSON.
THE ACT-DROP, ALSO BY Mr. STANFIELD, R.A.

AT THE END OF THE PLAY, HALF-AN-HOUR FOR REFRESHMENT.

To Conclude with Mrs. Inchbald's Farce, in Two Acts, of

ANIMAL MAGNETISM.

(THE SCENE IS LAID IN SEVILLE.)

THE DOCTOR	MR. CHARLES DICKENS.
PEDRILLO	MR. MARK LEMON.
THE MARQUIS DE LA GUARDIA	MR. YOUNG CHARLES.
GREGORIO	MR. WILKIE COLLINS.
CAMILLA	MISS KATE.
JACINTHA	MISS HOGARTH.

Musical Composer and Conductor of the Orchestra—Mr. FRANCESCO BERGER, who will preside at the Piano.

CARRIAGES MAY BE ORDERED AT HALF-PAST ELEVEN.

GOD SAVE THE QUEEN.

A private playbill for a performance at Dickens' house of *The Frozen Deep* on 6 January 1857. It was when he took this production on to the public stage to raise money for the family of Douglas Jerrold that Dickens first met Ellen Ternan. (With the permission of the Guildhall Museum)

to have serious consequences. Dickens broke with them for good, closed *Household Words* and fell out permanently with Mark Lemon, *Punch*'s editor and one of his oldest friends.

Dickens then wrote a second statement and sent it to Arthur Smith. Smith had managed the Jerrold fundraisers and also looked after the public readings that Dickens began at this time. This document was not a private letter but a semi-public justification (why send it to his manager of all people?). Whatever Dickens intended when he wrote what became known as the 'violated letter', it ended up in print. It was published in the *New York Tribune* in August 1858 and was soon copied in London. Dickens later exonerated Smith from any blame, but many friends and colleagues were dismayed at the tone Dickens had taken. Privately he was still seething and liable to intense cruelties, writing to Angela Burdett Coutts, after she had seen Catherine, that 'She does not – and she never did – care for the children: and the children do not – and they never did – care for her'.

After *The Frozen Deep*, Nelly and Maria went on to Doncaster to play there, and then to the Haymarket in London through until 1859. Dickens visited them. They lodged together until 1859, when Maria, together with her elder sister Fanny, took a long lease on a large house in Houghton Place. This property became Nelly's when she turned 21. No evidence suggests that she had come into any money, and certainly acting was not that lucrative. It is generally assumed that all of this was financed and stage-managed by Dickens. We are into a world of code (his accounts show payments to 'HP Trust'), conjecture and sudden invisibilities. Not least of Nelly herself, who disappears until a major event in 1865 jerks her back into the light.

• STAPLEHURST •

On 9 June 1865 there was a railway accident at Staplehurst in Kent. The bridge over the River Beult was being worked on and the track was up. Although it had all been planned to coincide with a gap in the timetable, the 'boat train' (which ran variably with the tide) had been forgotten. The train hit the gap and most of the carriages toppled off the bridge into the water. Ten people were killed and many more injured. In one of the remaining carriages sat Dickens, Nelly and her mother, shaken but physically largely unhurt. Dickens was alive to the danger of the situation in more ways than one and he made sure that Nelly and her mother made their safe exit away and up to

London before returning to retrieve the manuscript of the latest part of *Our Mutual Friend* and to comfort the injured. The accident haunted both Nelly (Dickens refers to her as 'the Patient' in surviving letters) and Dickens himself for some time. He was known to be nervous about travelling on trains in the future and he died on the anniversary of the crash five years later.

In her biography, Claire Tomalin studies the missing years before the accident through Dickens' movements. He is shown to be shuttling with hurried regularity between England and France. She suggests that Dickens set Nelly up in a house in France because she became pregnant and had a son, who died. It is certainly true that both Katey and Henry Dickens, many years later after Nelly's death, asserted that a boy was born to her, and their claims were published in a book of recollections compiled by Gladys Storey. Tomalin ties in a range of circumstantial evidence to suggest that this was the period when such an event happened.

• FINAL YEARS •

We know a bit more about what Dickens was up to in 1867 because when the year was nearly up he lost his diary. The little book was recovered and has been much pored over since. There are the towns he read in and the full names of his friends, but some entries are abbreviated to groups of letters or single letters. 'N' crops up quite a lot. So because of this diary, we know that Charles and Nelly started looking at houses in Peckham in June. In the end they settled on a property near Peckham Rye station: good access to the same London terminus that served Higham. It was called Windsor Lodge. The rates were subsequently paid by a man represented by a number of Dickens' aliases, which eventually evolved into 'Charles Tringham'.

Incredibly, especially considering all this secrecy, both Nelly and Dickens seem to have considered travelling to America (for the reading tour of 1867–68) together. At the very least, after Dickens' manager George Dolby had crossed the Atlantic first and warned them to be more circumspect, they had hopes of meeting up once the initial public acclaim had died down a little. The plan was that Dickens should send a coded message back to Nelly that she could interpret. 'All well' meant come; 'Safe and well' meant that she would have to stay put. Of course, once Dickens had arrived and spoken to his hosts, it became very clear that such a visit would not be possible. He sent the telegram to his friend W.H. Wills: 'Safe and well expect good letter full of hope.'

The strain of the American tour exacerbated a number of health problems. Dickens suffered from severe pains in his right foot and had to walk with a stick, limping through the UK tour that followed the American success. Then in Chester in 1869 he seems to have had a stroke. He wrote to his doctor describing symptoms of dizziness and numbness associated only with his left side. To Georgina, at Gad's Hill Place, he explained: 'My weakness and deadness are *on the left side*, and if I don't look at anything I try to touch with my left hand, I don't know where it is.'

That was the end of the tour. Perhaps to replace it, he soon began thinking about a new novel and started writing *The Mystery of Edwin Drood* in the autumn. In the event, even this new venture did not keep him from the stage – it merely added to his workload. He was back performing in January 1870, in London.

In 1870, shortly before he died, Dickens had a private interview with Queen Victoria, at her request. She wrote in her diary that he was 'very agreeable, with a pleasant voice and manner'. Dickens thought her 'strangely shy'. They talked about the assassination of President Lincoln, national education and the price of meat.

Dickens' Swiss chalet, where he wrote his last words. (Jeremy Clarke)

On 8 June at Gad's Hill, he worked hard on the novel, using Fechter's chalet across the road and extending his writing into the afternoon, contrary to his usual practice. When he met Georgina for dinner at six o'clock, he did not look well. He began to talk incoherently. She went to him and said, 'Come and lie down.' 'Yes,' he replied, 'on the ground.' Then he collapsed and lost consciousness. He never spoke again and died the following day.

PART 2

WRITING

6

A GUIDE TO THE NOVELS

· *THE PICKWICK PAPERS* ·

HOW AND WHEN?

First published in twenty instalments (as nineteen issues – the last was a double number) in 1836–37, illustrated by Robert Seymour, Robert Buss and Hablot Browne.

IN A SENTENCE?

A group of London stereotypes career hilariously around England smelling of the eighteenth century, exercising their leader's native benevolence but also winning him a dose of self-awareness (and immortality) at the hands of the Fleet prison and the best sidekick in the world.

GOOD THINGS?

No one put it better than G.K. Chesterton:

> ... before [Dickens] wrote a single real story, he had a kind of vision. It was a vision of the Dickens world – a maze of white roads, a map full of fantastic towns, thundering coaches, clamorous market-places, uproarious inns, strange and swaggering figures. That vision was Pickwick.

DISAPPOINTMENTS?

The Pickwick Papers is delightful, but it might be one of those books that is more enjoyable to re-read than to read. Its appeal can elude the first-timer, especially at the beginning. It helps not to expect a 'Victorian novel'.

READ ...

... to escape, wonderfully.

• *OLIVER TWIST* •

HOW AND WHEN?

Published in monthly parts in *Bentley's Miscellany* from February 1837 to April 1839. Illustrated by George Cruikshank.

IN A SENTENCE?

An abandoned orphan rejects the perilous excitements and vivid companionship of a life of crime for the solid middle-class existence for which he was secretly destined.

GOOD THINGS?

Fagin and his gang, the feeling of London, the Chertsey burglary and the murder itself are all unforgettable. The novel is also wonderfully strange: Oliver asleep dreaming of Monks and Fagin (who really are peering at him through a window); Oliver shut up alone, crouching 'in the corner of the passage by the street-door, to be as near living people as he could'; Sikes circling London, possessed by emptiness, 'idly breaking the hedges with his stick' while Nancy lies dead at home; Cruikshank's Oliver asking for more.

DISAPPOINTMENTS?

Although the book is subtitled '*The Parish Boy's Progress*', Oliver doesn't. His moral nature is never in doubt. Nancy and Rose Maylie are complimentary and unsatisfactory stereotypes. The plot creaks horribly: its needs produce Oliver's half-brother Monks, who is a figure of stage melodrama.

READ ...

... with astonishment.

• *NICHOLAS NICKLEBY* •

HOW AND WHEN?

Published in twenty monthly parts, as nineteen issues, in 1838–39. Illustrated by Hablot Browne.

IN A SENTENCE?

A dull young man rescues a disabled youth from an
evil school and together they embark on a series of
captivating adventures, leaving behind a life on the
stage to foil wicked plots and win love and riches (for
the dull young man).

GOOD THINGS?

Dotheboys Hall. Squeers is monster of the true
Dickensian type: horrifyingly alive. The scenes
amongst Vincent Crummles' touring company are
written with affection but with some sharpness too
and the author's vigorous enjoyment of them comes
through strongly. Wonderful minor characters are
everywhere: Mrs Nickleby, the Mantalinis, the
Kenwigses, Mr Lilyvick, Newman Noggs.

DISAPPOINTMENTS?

Those wonderful minor characters are balanced by
others who seem either inherited from cheap drama
(Sir Mulberry Hawk, Gride the miser) or almost
unnoticeably grey (Madeline Bray). The story is not
very important but this is just as well as it is not

very gripping. It is hard to care what happens to the eponymous hero.

... for the ensembles (families, schools, actors). And the funniest letter in English literature (chapter 15).

• *THE OLD CURIOSITY SHOP* •

HOW AND WHEN?

Published 1840–41 in weekly instalments (except for chapters 1 and 2, which were a month apart) within *Master Humphrey's Clock*, a miscellany dreamt up by Dickens for his publishers, Chapman and Hall, and edited by him. Illustrated by Samuel Williams, Daniel Maclise, George Cattermole and Hablot Browne.

IN A SENTENCE?

An angelic child and her feeble grandfather are pursued all over England by her enemies and his addiction, right into the embrace of death, so handing the hopeful reader over to a troglodyte servant and a bankrupt drunkard, who defeat the dwarf and love each other.

GOOD THINGS?

A bewildering car crash of anti-modern folk meanings with the monsters of the nineteenth-century city. A fairy tale, with wanderings, wilderness and a sleeping beauty who really does go to sleep forever. Also very funny and occasionally alarming.

DISAPPOINTMENTS?

It all depends how you end up taking it. Nell's death was originally a sensation, then became notorious as an example of Dickens' peculiar weaknesses: idealisation (of young women, especially) and sentimentality. The novel was originally improvised from something like a sketch or short story, and this shows throughout.

READ …

… because nobody ever wrote like this before and nobody will do so again.

• *BARNABY RUDGE* •

HOW AND WHEN?

The second novel from the *Master Humphrey's Clock* experiment. Long contemplated, *Barnaby Rudge* was eventually published in weekly parts from February to November 1841. Illustrated by George Cattermole and Hablot Browne.

IN A SENTENCE?

Barnaby, a fatherless youth with some unspecified mental disability, lives in a community at the heart of which lies the Maypole Inn, whose members are drawn into the London anti-Catholic riots of 1780, during which he is adopted as a mascot by a people's army that burns its way into Newgate prison, there uncovering his criminal father but implicating him in an act for which he is condemned to death and later pardoned, although the Maypole is burned and the hangman hanged.

GOOD THINGS?

The riots are a tour de force and very gripping. The interpenetration of fiction and fact is skilfully managed. The Maypole Inn is a wonderful example of

Dickens' living buildings; its destruction is peculiarly shocking. Dolly Varden is perhaps more appealing than some of Dickens' other heroines.

DISAPPOINTMENTS?

Never one of Dickens' most admired works. The mystery of Barnaby's father and his crime is not very mysterious and becomes tedious quickly. With Sir John Chester, Dickens seems to be trying too hard and he is not convincing. Overall, perhaps lacks a certain Dickensian spark.

READ ...

... so you can burn down Newgate prison. 'I have let all the prisoners out of Newgate, burnt down Lord Mansfield's, and played the very devil ... I feel quite smoky when I am at work,' wrote Dickens to Forster.

• MARTIN CHUZZLEWIT •

HOW AND WHEN?

Published in monthly parts, as nineteen issues, in 1843–44. Illustrated by Hablot Browne.

IN A SENTENCE?

A selfish young man takes on America in order to spite his grandfather and fail to make his fortune, while back home his scheming ex-tutor falls into the clutches of a swindler and a murderer (of the swindler), before returning to marry appropriately and be happy.

GOOD THINGS?

Still crackles with the unrestrainable brilliance of the early Dickens, although here he is beginning to tie things to an overarching theme. Mrs Gamp and Pecksniff are pure gold and as funny as anything Dickens ever wrote. Todgers, the boarding house where the Pecksniffs stay on their visit to London, is hallowed Dickensian territory. The American episodes are written with enormous verve (the memories were fresh) and the emblematic feel of the journey to the wretched settlement of Eden comes through strongly.

DISAPPOINTMENTS?

Ruth Pinch. Dickens loves her too much. Tom Pinch is almost as difficult for a modern reader to keep down. Young Martin becomes a mere device at times during the American scenes, instead of a convincing individual, and his moral conversion is perhaps a little complete and abrupt. The book is long and rambling.

READ …

… for the extremes. Fantastic hilarity and delight with the magical Mrs Gamp; cringe-worthy thigh-rubbing and leering over Ruth Pinch; and perhaps the most shocking moment in the whole of the Dickens canon as Jonas Chuzzlewit is discovered having failed to commit suicide at the first attempt.

• DOMBEY AND SON •

HOW AND WHEN?

Published in twenty monthly parts, as nineteen issues, in 1846–48. Illustrated by Hablot Browne.

IN A SENTENCE?

A rich widower loses his son and embarks on a heartless second marriage before being betrayed and losing everything except the love of the daughter he has despised.

GOOD THINGS?

Rich and suggestive, and full of contemporary resonance: railways, capitalism, empire, gender and sexuality. Paul Dombey's short life is described partly in compelling child's-eye view, and his schooldays introduce some wonderful comedy. Dickens' picture of Florence, although of a piece with his other ideal heroines, works rather better here because of how we understand her nature is crushed under the eye of her father. A novel that lingers in the mind. Great illustrations.

DISAPPOINTMENTS?

Edith Dombey is a serious weakness. The novel deserves her to be better than a figure that shares so much with popular melodrama.

READ …

… and feel Victorian Britain getting to know itself.

• DAVID COPPERFIELD •

HOW AND WHEN?

Published in twenty monthly parts, as nineteen issues, in 1849–50. Illustrated by Hablot Browne.

IN A SENTENCE?

David grows to maturity surviving abuse at the hands of his stepfather, a ghastly school, indigent friends and degrading labour, while adoring older boy Steerforth, to whom he introduces his childhood sweetheart, thus ruining her; falls in love himself, marries, repents, grieves, sees Steerforth die and gets married again –

Ivorex plaque of Uriah Heep, from *David Copperfield*. (With the permission of the Guildhall Museum)

to his friend and counsellor after helping to rescue her father from villainy and becoming a famous writer.

GOOD THINGS?

The first quarter or so – David's childhood, the days at Mr Creakle's school, the Micawbers – is a thing to marvel at. And much of the novel continues to delight: there is Mr Dick, the 'mad' companion and adviser of Aunt Betsey; Mrs Crupp, David's landlady; and there are episodes such as David getting drunk and his later attempts at making a home with Dora. Great pictures, again.

DISAPPOINTMENTS?

After such a beginning, there is an inevitable slight falling away. Dickens' handling of the sexual issues raised in the novel is not a success. Martha, the 'fallen' woman who comes good, is a Victorian stereotype born out of a kind of moral wishful thinking. And the Doctor Strong sub-plot, in which the elderly head-master is led to believe his young wife is unfaithful, is just ghastly. Agnes is not great, either.

READ ...

... for the eerie magic Dickens works as he shuts us in the house with David and Mr Murdstone. Fascinating and terrifying.

• *BLEAK HOUSE* •

HOW AND WHEN?

Published in twenty monthly parts, as nineteen issues, in 1852–53. Illustrated by Hablot Browne.

IN A SENTENCE?

Brought up in disgrace and determined to be useful, Esther Summerson devotes herself to her guardian, supports her new friends through a notorious legal case, works hard and falls ill before discovering the mystery of her birth only at the expense of her mother's life; once recovered she is released from the duty of marrying her guardian to marry whom she chooses.

GOOD THINGS?

Huge and extensive, but dense, and of an immensely fine texture. At times marvellously dark. A muscular plot, whose coincidences show how we are all impossibly inextricably linked to and (therefore) responsible for one another. Astonishingly, considering Dickens' record with heroines, Esther's narrative works fairly well, and its relationship with the 'other' narrator's manner adds great richness to the reader's experience. Hablot Browne's 'dark' plates – the gloomy pictures that crop up in the second half of the novel – are wonderfully complementary.

DISAPPOINTMENTS?

None. Of course, it is long and complex and there is some moral grandstanding. That's kind of the point.

READ …

… just read. Or read it again.

• HARD TIMES •

HOW AND WHEN?

Published in 1854 as twenty weekly instalments in *Household Words*, Dickens' own magazine.

IN A SENTENCE?

A man sees his children ruined by the comprehensive failure of his system of guidance and discipline, being saved, if he is saved, only by the intervention of despised outsiders and the exposure of the hypocritical friend to whom he had sacrificed his daughter.

GOOD THINGS?

The beginning; the circus community; Sissy and her father; Bounderby, the 'bully of humility'. Louisa is one of the more interesting of Dickens' female principals. He practises a sort of economy which is generally quite effective.

DISAPPOINTMENTS?

The portrait of the trade union activist, Slackbridge, is heavy-handed. It makes us suspicious of Dickens' apolitical solutions to class antagonism. Stephen and Rachael are rather colourless.

READ ...

... to see a different kind of Dickens that kind of works.

• *LITTLE DORRIT* •

HOW AND WHEN?

Published in twenty monthly parts, as nineteen issues, in 1855–57. Illustrated by Hablot Browne.

IN A SENTENCE?

Amy Dorrit, a child born in the Marshalsea gaol, steers her father through the everyday humiliations of prison life until he is freed into the greater prison of the world, loses his mind and dies, giving Amy a chance to save her beloved, but broken and bankrupt,

Arthur Clennam, who can only accept her love once his own sinister family mysteries are solved.

GOOD THINGS?

The book is held together by its central theme, and by the restrained presentation of Clennam's troubles. Full of unforgettable characters – again. Amy Dorrit? An individual traumatised by years of sacrifice finally allowed a possibility of self-assertion in the carefully elevated ending.

DISAPPOINTMENTS?

The Clennam plot is almost unfathomable and not remotely convincing. Rigaud is silly. Amy Dorrit? Another idealised Dickens heroine as infantile as she is dutiful.

READ ...

... to be on the inside.

Dickens in 1858, with eleven full-length novels behind him and about to embark on *A Tale of Two Cities*, an extraordinary public reading career and a new life in the country. (With the permission of the Guildhall Museum)

• *A Tale of Two Cities* •

How and when?

Published as weekly instalments in *All the Year Round*, Dickens' magazine, in 1859 (and also in monthly parts later that year). The monthly parts were illustrated by Hablot Browne.

In a sentence?

A dissolute but able lawyer devotes himself to a young woman whose father becomes a French revolutionary hero upon his release from prison, and seizes his moment during the Terror, when her husband is condemned to death in France, by swapping places with him and going to the guillotine in his place.

Good things?

The living/dead Dr Manette is a haunting portrait of a damaged individual. There are some grand set pieces.

Disappointments?

A little flat.

READ ...

... and marvel at why this one is so well known.

• *GREAT EXPECTATIONS* •

HOW AND WHEN?

Published as weekly instalments in *All the Year Round* in 1860–61.

IN A SENTENCE?

Pip remembers: coming into a mysterious fortune as a child, becoming a 'gentleman' and abandoning his family, before discovering that his great benefactor was not the local eccentric but an escaped criminal he saved, who returns to claim his affection, which Pip in extremity eventually gives, forgiving him and himself and old love Estella who has despised him and to whom he at last returns, perhaps.

GOOD THINGS?

Precisely realised but sweepingly universal. Effortlessly hits the big themes of self-determination, social complicity, guilt, memory and class identity. Hugely resonant. Also funny, sinister and incredibly exciting. Held together by Pip's reflective tone and the patterns and associations that run through the book.

DISAPPOINTMENTS?

Try to get a sight of the original ending. What do you think?

READ …

… lots.

• *OUR MUTUAL FRIEND* •

HOW AND WHEN?

Published as twenty monthly parts, as nineteen issues, in 1864–65. Illustrated by Marcus Stone.

IN A SENTENCE?

When its heir is found dead, a fortune built on rubbish goes to an illiterate old servant, who takes in the heir's betrothed and assumes an evil character to teach her a lesson and outwit his enemies, while a dissolute young lawyer pursues the daughter of a waterman, is almost murdered, is saved and marries her, as the heir reveals himself alive in the midst of all to claim his double reward.

GOOD THINGS?

Marvellously poised between the filthy rich and the filthy who are rich. Odd (Jenny Wren, the dolls' dressmaker), funny (the Wilfers), odd and funny (Mr Venus). Like a fable, but crouched down in the dirt of everyday life, in the classic Dickens manner.

DISAPPOINTMENTS?

The mix of the fabulous and the realistic can lead to some uncomfortable moments.

READ ...

... if you want it all: social satire, domestic comedy, mystery, romance, symbolism, madness and marriages.

• *THE MYSTERY OF EDWIN DROOD* •

HOW AND WHEN?

Unfinished novel published in six monthly parts in 1870. Charles Collins designed the monthly wrapper, but the novel was illustrated by Luke Fildes.

IN A SENTENCE?

John Jasper, opium user and choirmaster, loving his nephew but loving his nephew's fiancée more, and taking an unhealthy interest both in the hidden places of Cloisterham Cathedral and in engineering a general antagonism to recent arrivals from abroad, gets a double shock; 'discovers' his nephew's disappearance and the friendly dissolution of his engagement.

GOOD THINGS?

A wonderfully sleepy, creepy picture of Cloisterham adds great depth to the action.

DISAPPOINTMENTS?

Even when you know it's coming, it still hurts to see the blank page and put the book down.

The sleepy old Rochester of Dickens' memory – and *The Mystery of Edwin Drood*. An engraving published in 1820. (With the permission of the Guildhall Museum)

READ ...

... to wonder, of course, but also to see Dickens assimilating new literary fashions.

7

SHORTER FICTION

• BOOKS •

The only problem talking about Dickens' shorter
books – those works that fit between his big novels
and his magazine stories – is that in 1843 he wrote the
greatest short work of prose fiction in the English language, probably in any language, probably ever. This,
of course, was *A Christmas Carol*. For many readers this
book epitomises Dickens' entire output, not just his
shorter works, such is the affection in which it is held.

• A CHRISTMAS CAROL •

HOW AND WHEN?

Published in a single volume on 19 December 1843. Although it was immediately successful, Dickens spent a frustrating few months failing to realise any substantial profits (the first edition, with colour pictures, was very expensive to produce) and taking the publishers of a plagiarised version to court. He won the case, but ended up paying all costs when the offending individuals declared bankruptcy.

IN A SENTENCE?

Hard-hearted Scrooge hates Christmas and begrudges the day off he has to give his clerk, but is saved by the night-time intervention of three spirits, who work on his memory and revive his compassion, so that he awakes on Christmas morning to treat the deserving and celebrate with his family.

GOOD THINGS?

They abound. Brings together Dickens' interest in 'fireside storytelling', his clever manipulation of character types and his concern for contemporary social issues. All this and the best beginning ever.

DISAPPOINTMENTS?

Not a trace.

READ …

… to share in it.

• OTHER CHRISTMAS BOOKS •

Such was the *Carol*'s success that Dickens published four more single-volume prose fictions in the 1840s, works that today are generally known as the 'Christmas Books'. Even though they do not all take place at that time of year, they showcase what Dickens himself came to think of as his '*Carol* philosophy'.

The Chimes (1844) tells the story of a poor ageing porter who is convinced of the inescapably bad nature of all poor people by the bullying and invective of a number of authority figures. He falls asleep in a church and is persuaded otherwise by the spirits of the bells, awakening the following morning to join the wedding preparations of his daughter.

In *The Cricket on the Hearth* (1845), which, interestingly, was subtitled *A Fairy Tale of Home*, the agent of change is a cricket that sings next to the fireplace and stands for all that is sacred to the family. In the story, a husband becomes suspicious of his wife as she is seen talking to a stranger. All ends happily.

In *The Battle of Life* (1846), the close relationship between two sisters leads one, Marion, to sacrifice her lover to the other, Grace, because she knows that Grace secretly loves him. Marion's selfless behaviour rescues her father from his own ingrained and complacent cynicism.

The Haunted Man (1848) is a scholar named Redlaw, who has become sadly embittered by his past life. In a twist on the *Carol* formula, he is offered release from his memories via a supernatural agency that will bring him forgetfulness. This, however, makes him a savage who blights the life of everyone with whom he comes into contact. He is redeemed at the end of the book through the kind offices of Milly, the wife of the lodge keeper at his college.

THE CHRISTMAS STORIES

Another format replaced the Christmas Books at the beginning of the 1850s. Dickens decided to use his position as editor of the magazines *Household Words* and then *All the Year Round* to establish an annual Christmas number. This idea really caught on and the Christmas edition became something of a 'special', growing in size eventually to forty-eight pages. The advantage of rehearsing the '*Carol* philosophy' through a magazine format was that it could become a corporate enterprise, with contributions from other writers. Dickens usually liked a central theme or scenario that bound the stories together. In 1862, for instance, the linking device was the discovery of an unclaimed piece of luggage that contained a series of manuscript stories.

This takes us back to the beginning of Dickens' career and the magazine that produced *The Old Curiosity Shop* and *Barnaby Rudge – Master Humphrey's Clock*. Master Humphrey liked to gather his friends around an old grandfather clock whose case contained contributions from the circle, which were read to the assembled company. This is important because it reminds us of Dickens' continuing attachment to storytelling and sharing, its link to memories of the dying year and the promise of renewal. In some ways the content of the stories are of marginal importance (they are certainly not all Christmassy); it was the act of telling that was the key.

Despite their manageable size, the Christmas stories receive much less attention than the big novels these days. Many are rather sentimental. The framework for the stories in 1855, for example, was 'The Holly Tree Inn', in which several travellers were trapped by the weather. Dickens' contributions included that of the 'Boots' (a servant) at the inn, who tells the story of two young children who innocently run away to get married at Gretna Green.

However, 1863 gave us Mrs Lirriper – by any account one of Dickens' most exuberant voices. Mrs Lirriper, a widow, keeps lodgings and rattles through her tale without sparing a host of incidental – not to say bizarre – details. The story is sentimental in content (she adopts a baby whose unmarried mother dies in her house), but by assuming the voice somehow Dickens finds a kind of discipline and the result is very moving. She speaks as if the reader is sitting in her house:

I am an old woman now and my good looks are gone but that's me my dear over the plate-warmer and considered like in the times when you used to pay two guineas on ivory and took your chance pretty much how you came out, which made you very careful how you left it about afterwards because people were turned so red and uncomfortable by mostly guessing it was somebody else quite different, and there was once a certain person that had put his money in a hop business that came in one morning to pay his rent and his respects being the second floor that would have taken it down from its hook and put it in his breast-pocket – you understand my dear – for the L, he says of the original – only there was no mellowness in HIS voice and I wouldn't let him, but his opinion of it you may gather from his saying to it 'Speak to me Emma!' which was far from a rational observation no doubt but still a tribute to its being a likeness, and I think myself it WAS like me when I was young and wore that sort of stays.

For the 1866 number of *All the Year Round*, Dickens produced 'The Signalman', a deservedly well-known ghost story, in which a lone railway worker appears to foresee disasters.

8

JOURNALISM

· DICKENS AS A JOURNALIST ·

Dickens the journalist did not cease to exist after the publication of his magazine work of the 1830s. The sketches and stories written as 'Boz', lively and clever though they were, were only the beginning of his work in this area. In fact, there is hardly any separating the novelist from the journalist: both wrote for magazines; both employed acute observation of places and people; both relied heavily on personal memory; both made things up.

John Forster was on the staff of the *Examiner* weekly newspaper from 1836, and served as its editor between 1847 and 1855. This provided Dickens with a further outlet for his journalism. He contributed reviews of plays and books and he wrote to comment on the current affairs of the day. Broadly speaking, the political thinking he displayed was in line with the *Examiner*'s reputation as a liberal, reforming paper. In April 1848, for instance, he was inspired by the statistics released by the government 'in reference to the alliance of crime with ignorance'. His piece 'Ignorance and Crime' attacks the 'state of mental confusion' that is 'commonly called "education" in England', especially the complacent role in it played by religious organisations.

He always had it in for those who would impose a moral system upon the poor without any consideration of how the financial and social pressures of their lives affected their behaviour. Although he found his old friend Cruikshank's work as powerful as ever in the 1840s, he felt uncomfortable about his wholesale conversion to the temperance movement and the way he employed his talents (and used his name) to support the cause. So when Cruikshank produced a sequel to *The Bottle*, his enormously popular anti-alcohol illustrated sequence, Dickens cried foul. In his review, he wrote: 'Few men have a better right to erect themselves into teachers of the people than Mr George Cruikshank … But this teaching, to last, must be fairly conducted.'

Of the gin shop, Dickens claims that: 'Drunkenness does not begin there. It has a teeming and reproachful history anterior to that stage; and at the remediable evil in that history, it is the duty of the moralist, if he strikes at all, to strike deep and spare not.'

The problem with *The Bottle* was the sleight of hand that concentrated the whole shocking power of its subjects' decline on a single sip of drink. Dickens spotted that, of course. Its hero:

> lived in undoubted comfort and good esteem until he was some five-and-thirty years of age, when, happening, unluckily, to have a goose for dinner one day, in the bosom of his thriving family, he jocularly sent out for a bottle of gin, and persuaded his wife (until then a pattern of neatness and good housewifery) to take a little drop, after the stuffing; from which moment the family never left off drinking gin, and rushed downhill to destruction, very fast.

Perhaps most famously, Dickens used the pages of the *Examiner* to publicise the case of Bartholomew Drouet's baby 'farm' in 'The Paradise at Tooting'. Drouet undertook to take children from a number of workhouse authorities in London and contracted to keep them for a fee of 4*s* 6*d* per head per week. This was a common (though notorious) practice – Dickens refers to it in *Oliver Twist*. But Drouet's establishment was huge: it housed 1,300 children. Despite warnings from the newly formed Board of Health, cholera broke out there in 1848 and children began to die in very large numbers. At first, incredibly, the Surrey coroner saw no need to hold an inquest and, when finally the law intervened, there was a panic to shift the blame. Dickens refers to these events at the beginning of his article, and to the subsequent report that exposed the appalling conditions in the house. His tone is withering:

Of all similar establishments on earth, that at Tooting was the most admirable. Of all similar contractors on earth, Mr Drouet was the most disinterested, zealous, and unimpeachable. Of all the wonders ever wondered at, nothing perhaps had ever occurred more wonderful than the outbreak and rapid increase of a disorder so horrible, in a place so perfectly regulated. There was no warning of its approach. Nothing was less to be expected. The farmed children were slumbering in the lap of peace and plenty … when, in a moment, the destroyer was upon them, and Tooting churchyard became too small for the piles of children's coffins that were carried out of this Elysium every day.

Dickens then methodically proceeds to dismantle the ironic picture here presented. He spreads the blame wider and condemns inspectors and poor law guardians who allowed Drouet to supply rotten food and not even enough of that; house sick children four to a bed in filthy conditions; clothe them in the middle of winter in flannel garments that could be 'read through'; and intimidate any children who seemed likely to complain. It is strong stuff. And ends without equivocation:

> The cholera, or some unusually malignant form of typhus assimilating itself to that disease, broke out in Mr Drouet's farm for children, because it was brutally conducted, vilely kept, preposterously inspected, dishonestly defended, a disgrace to a Christian community, and a stain upon a civilised land.

• DICKENS AS AN EDITOR •

Our idea of Dickens' journalistic activity is complicated by his involvement in what was essentially a corporate practice, by being in charge of a team, commissioning and correcting (and sometimes rewriting). By being, of course, an editor. Dickens' career as an editor of newspapers and magazines was one to which he devoted an enormous amount of time and energy.

He received invaluable assistance on his own magazines from W.H. Wills, who managed much of the business side of the publications and indeed, in Dickens' last years, dealt with many personal matters for him too.

> *Dickens edited the memoirs of Joseph Grimaldi, perhaps the most famous clown who ever lived.*

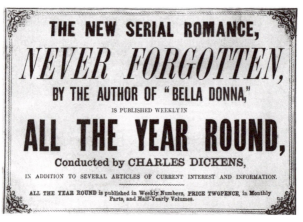

An advert for *All the Year Round* highlighting a new story beginning in September 1864. *Never Forgotten* was written by Percy Fitzgerald, a man who later donated his collection of Dickens material to the Rochester Museum. (With the permission of the Guildhall Museum)

THE DAILY NEWS

In 1845 Dickens' publishers, Bradbury and Evans, proposed to him that he become the editor of a brand new newspaper, which was to be of liberal politics and of a stature to rival *The Times*. Once Dickens agreed, he was given a free hand (and a large salary) to hire the best reporters and writers of the day. Perhaps surprisingly, one of these was Dickens' own father, who had been a fearful (and financial) nuisance to Dickens throughout his growing career (but who remained faithful to his work at the *Daily News* until he died in 1851). The first edition was full of mistakes and Dickens had to insert a letter into the next issue with an apology. In fact, he remained editor only for about three weeks before handing it over to John Forster. The paper did carry a few significant contributions by him, however, most notably a number of letters appealing for the abolition of the death penalty. He also submitted a series of articles called 'Travelling

In 1840 Dickens witnessed a public execution and was so appalled by the spectacle that he wrote a series of campaigning letters to the **Daily News** *calling for the total abolition of the death penalty.*

Letters Written on the Road', describing a journey through France and Italy.

HOUSEHOLD WORDS

Household Words was a weekly magazine, part owned by Dickens, edited by him and for which he wrote stories and non-fiction. It ran from 1850 to 1859 and cost 2*d*. Everything in it was published anonymously, including material by writers with a reputation already established elsewhere. Some articles were collaborations. The range of subjects covered was huge, taking in science, geography and history, as well as short fiction. There was also a campaigning element and the magazine contributed to contemporary debates about housing, education and crime. It was a great success and sold steadily, finding a loyal middle-class readership.

A change in policy came for the magazine in 1854, with the inclusion of the first piece of serialised long fiction, Dickens' own *Hard Times*, which ran for twenty instalments until August that year. Its concern with industrial unrest, education, popular entertainment and the treatment of workers made it a good fit with the general tone of the magazine. In fact, Dickens was careful to judge each issue as a whole, and often remarks on his editorial balancing act in letters to friends. *Household Words* ended rather abruptly in 1859 because Dickens fell out with his co-owners and publishers, Bradbury and Evans. After a short court case, he wound up the magazine, although he was far from finished with weekly periodicals.

ALL THE YEAR ROUND

All the Year Round survived Dickens and carried some of his best-known fiction. It outsold *Household Words* and the sales figures for its Christmas numbers were enormous. We know less about how the magazine was managed by Dickens and his sub-editor, Wills, as the records that survive for *Household Words* are lost. It is sometimes said that the quality is not so good, despite the magazine's popularity and the important fiction – from Dickens, but also from Elizabeth Gaskell and Wilkie Collins – it consciously set out to bring before the public. Its articles certainly have less to say about current affairs. The publication of *Great Expectations* in the magazine is a good example both of how closely Dickens kept in touch with his readers, and how boldly he could act to keep them. After *A Tale of Two Cities* had been published in the magazine during 1859, Dickens later moved on to give 'headline status' to a novel by Charles Lever, called *A Day's Ride*. Sales fell to disappointing levels and, having already begun to draft *Great Expectations* as another big, twenty-month part work, Dickens decided to refashion his opening and convert the new novel into a weekly. Lever was relegated to the inside pages, and the first instalment of *Great Expectations* appeared in December 1860. The novel we have today would have been quite different given the space available in the extended format. *All the Year Round* was finally wound up by Dickens' son Charley in 1895.

9

SUBJECTS & THEMES

· LONDON ·

Perhaps London was Dickens' greatest subject. He lived there, of course, and some of his most important London years were spent wandering its streets as a child, taking it all in, storing away all those fine impressions for later use. London was an awakening, and a harsh one too, after the idyllic childhood spent in the Medway towns. In London he became a man, learned about work, tasted loneliness and want and shame. But London also saw him embark upon family life and independence; it became full of friends and laughter; it was inspiration – as necessary to his art as pen and paper. If Chatham was 'the birthplace of his fancy' (John Forster), then London was the cradle of his success.

LONDON AS NOURISHMENT

The city is a major part of all Dickens' novels, except *Hard Times*. He seemed to need it artistically, not simply as a context in which things could take place, but as a growing medium out of which the stories and characters sprang. He wrote to Forster from Genoa about his frustration about being away and trying to work: 'I seem as if I have plucked myself out of my proper soil ... and could take root no more until I return to it.'

If Dickens needed London, London equally needed him. There is a sense in which Dickens' uncanny mixture of observation and imagination, his ability to watch and typify, told Londoners who they were. He gave a name to that thing Londoners felt – the change, the distinctiveness, the fearful precipitate activity of the city – and made them feel that they were part of something that made sense, because it could be described. This is particularly the case in the *Sketches*, with their accounts of cabs, omnibuses, steamboats, gin shops and pleasure gardens; but it remains true to the end.

LONDON VARIOUS

> Draw but a little circle above the clustering housetops,
> and you shall have within its space everything, with its
> opposite extreme and contradiction close beside.

Dickens' Master Humphrey (from his weekly periodical *Master Humphrey's Clock*) here describes one of the functional aspects of the London universe that made it so useful for such a writer. An entire world in a street, its individual parts forced into neighbourhood, in ignorance of the lives that teemed perpetually within arm's length – here was a scene to work on. Here, 'life and death went hand-in-hand; wealth and poverty stood side-by-side' (*Nicholas Nickleby*). For Dickens this combination of closeness, blindness and difference stirred his talents in all kinds of ways. The 'closeness' promoted the accidental happenings that are so vital to Dickens' art: the coincidental fertility of paths crossing, of discovery and change. The 'blindness' stirred Dickens' indignation and led him to foreground peripheral figures of the streets like Jo the crossing sweeper, ever present but always ignored. The 'difference' he used to underline the essential humanity that joins us together – as in *Bleak House* the disease that afflicts Jo is brought to Esther too:

How many people may there be in London, who, if we had brought them deviously and blindfold, to this street … would know it for a not remote part of the city in which their lives are passed? How many, who, amidst this compound of sickening smells, these heaps of filth, these tumbling houses, with all their vile contents, animate and inanimate, slimily over-flowing into the black road, would believe that they breathe this air?

THE LONDON CROWD

Dickens was a great identifier of the distinctive and eccentric, but he was also an adept observer of crowds, and 'the crowd'. He can define and manip-ulate a mob within a narrative like a character, its individuals acting like parts from a whole. This is Newgate prison, burning, in *Barnaby Rudge*:

Although the heat was so intense that the paint on the houses over against the prison, parched and crackled up, and swelling into boils, as it were from excess of torture, broke and crumbled away; although the glass fell from the window-sashes, and the lead and iron on the roofs blistered the incautious hand that touched them, and the sparrows in the eaves took wing, and rendered giddy by the smoke, fell fluttering down upon the blazing pile; still the fire was tended unceasingly by busy hands, and round it, men were going always. They never slackened in their zeal, or kept aloof, but pressed upon the flames so hard, that those in front had much ado to save themselves from being thrust in; if one man swooned or dropped, a dozen struggled for his place, and that although they knew the pain, and thirst, and pressure to be unendurable. Those who fell down in fainting-fits, and were not crushed or burnt, were carried to an inn-yard close at hand, and dashed with water from a pump; of which buckets full were passed from man to man among the crowd; but such was the strong desire of all to drink, and such the fighting to be first, that, for the most part, the whole contents were spilled upon the ground, without the lips of one man being moistened.

Or he can suddenly produce a crowd from nowhere, from what was a moment ago a disparate collection of people, forced into being by some event, exciting or dismal or both. The 'red cab' of the *Sketches* has had an accident:

You had hardly turned into the street, when you saw a trunk or two, lying on the ground: an uprooted post, a hat-box, a portmanteau, and a carpet-bag, strewed about in a very picturesque manner: a horse in a cab standing by, looking about him with great unconcern; and a crowd, shouting and screaming with delight, cooling their flushed faces against the glass windows of a chemist's shop. – 'What's the matter here, can you tell me?' – 'O'ny a cab, sir.' – 'Anybody hurt, do you know?' – 'O'ny the fare, sir. I see him a turnin' the corner, and I ses to another gen'lm'n "that's a reg'lar little oss that, and he's a comin' along rayther sweet, an't he?" – "He just is," ses the other gen'lm'n, ven bump they cums agin the post, and out flies the fare like bricks.'

• JOBS & JOBBING •

Dickens' reporter's eye and his performer's talent for mimicry come together most wonderfully in the notice he takes of professional behaviours. Some of his most famous characters are strongly identified with what they do for a living. This is Dickens territory: the place where individuals become types and types behave like individuals. Dickens picks apart the assumptions we make about people from the tiniest aspects of their behaviour and examines where those ticks and habits come from. Here is the life that is lived, the feeling of things being done, giving texture to Dickens' narrative.

WAITERS

There was no escaping the tyranny of personal attendance in the Victorian period, whether you were one of those serving or those served. Today we associate service with eating out. But waiters might also serve customers off the premises or fetch and carry from tavern to home. Many single gentlemen would have no facilities for cooking so would buy in food and help. There was the coaching stop too. Before the railway, travelling long distance meant enforced use of roadside taverns and hotels, where catching the eye of the staff as you alighted might get you the warmest spot in the house. In these interactions there is much room for comedy.

Waiters, of course, look for an opportunity to serve because that is how they make money: in Dickens' inns and hotels if they are not in full view, they are always round the corner, within earshot. Dickens writes of waiters 'consenting' to leave the room when they are not wanted. In 'The Great Winglebury Duel', in *Sketches by Boz*, we see a waiter run through his exit routine:

The waiter pulled down the window-blind, and then pulled it up again – for a regular waiter must do something before he leaves the room – adjusted the glasses on the side-board, brushed a place that was NOT dusty, rubbed his hands very hard, walked stealthily to the door, and evaporated.

UNDERTAKERS

Dickens' undertakers are immersed in the paraphernalia of their trade. When Pip, in *Great Expectations*, returns home from London for his sister's funeral, he finds the house has been taken over by Mr Trabb, the undertaker, who is managing the whole thing. He prepares the ribbons, crepe and wrappings that are worn by the close family. Or, as Pip says, as his sister's body is carried out of the house: 'We were all going to "follow", and were all in course of being tied up separately … into ridiculous bundles.' The grieving family emerge from their home: 'Pocket handkerchiefs out, all!' cries Trabb.

Mr Sowerberry, in *Oliver Twist*, is almost relentlessly affable. He uses a snuffbox which is in the shape of a coffin. He regrets that fat people who are taken into the workhouse die so quickly, before they have been starved thin, as it means a more expensive box.

Dickens was fascinated by death and dead people, but repelled by ostentatious funerals. In his will, he gave strict instructions for his own. He ordered that he was to be 'buried in an inexpensive, unostentatious and strictly private manner ... and that those attending my funeral wear no scarf, cloak, black bow, long hat-band, or other such revolting absurdity'.

His shop is 'close and hot' and it smells 'of coffins'. Mr Sowerberry has a business interest in Oliver and takes him out of parish care. His plan is to use the boy as a 'mute': a silent mourner provided as a funeral service. It works a treat:

In commercial phrase, coffins were looking up; and, in the course of a few weeks, Oliver acquired a great deal of experience ... many were the mournful processions that little Oliver headed, in a hat-band reaching down to his knees, to the indescribable emotion of all the mothers in the town.

LAWYERS

As a young man Dickens worked as a clerk with two firms of solicitors. He worked as a law reporter, transcribing case details for the newspapers. He registered as a student barrister in 1839 (resigning in 1855, without having practised). And when he married Catherine, they went to live in Furnival's Inn, part of the traditional home of the English law. It seems hardly surprising that the law and lawyers feature strongly in his writing. Indeed, *Bleak House* is about the law.

The picture is rarely complimentary. Mr Pickwick's solicitor, Mr Perker, may seem approachable, but the barrister he employs on his client's behalf, Serjeant Snubbin, is an embodiment of the irretrievably dusty, impenetrable dense legal environment that Dickens is to revisit later in his career:

He had that dull-looking boiled eye which is often to be seen in the heads of people who have applied themselves during many years to a weary and laborious course of study ... His hair was thin and weak, which was partly attributable to his having never devoted much time to its arrangement, and partly to his having worn for five-and-twenty years the forensic wig which hung on a block beside him. The marks of hair-powder on his coat-collar, and the ill-washed and worse tied white neckerchief round his throat, showed that he had not found leisure since he left the court to make any alteration in his dress: while the slovenly style of the remainder of his costume warranted the inference that his personal appearance would not have been very much improved if he had.

The sinister aspects of this world are brought to the fore in *Bleak House*, which features Mr Tulkinghorn, attorney to the titled world, who 'is indifferent to everything but his calling. His calling is the acquisition of secrets, and the holding possession of such power as they give him.'

CAB DRIVERS

Cabs were part of the rattling backdrop to life in London. With two wheels and a single seat for a passenger, they were about as small as a horse-drawn vehicle could very well be – for squeezing through and around the terrible traffic that afflicted the city.

Mr Pickwick has trouble with a cab driver at the very beginning of his travels. Once the cabman has been called (from the pub), 'Mr Pickwick and his portmanteau were thrown into the vehicle'. The proximity of driver and passenger (they sit side by side) allows the cabman to indulge in a deadpan series of preposterous statements, which Mr Pickwick takes down as facts, and 'as a singular instance of the tenacity of life in horses, under trying circumstances'. The Pickwick notebook, however, causes offence. Even the three Pickwickian friends who are waiting to receive their leader seem a suspicious occurrence. The cab driver labels Mr Pickwick an informer: '… arter agger-awatin' me to assault him, [he] gets three witnesses here to prove it. But I'll give it him, if I've six months for it.'

Then, 'sparring like clockwork', he proceeds to take them all on. Only the arrival of Mr Jingle spares the Pickwickians further embarrassment and injury.

It is a cab driver who features in one of the funniest of the *Sketches*. The 'red cab' is a lethal conveyance that Dickens pictures laying a trail of destruction throughout the city, and entertaining the rubber-necking crowd with its antics. We get a good look at the cab driver himself:

He was a brown-whiskered, white-hatted, no-coated cabman; his nose was generally red, and his bright blue eye not unfrequently stood out in bold relief against a black border of artificial workmanship; his boots were of the Wellington form, pulled up to meet his corduroy knee-smalls, or at least to approach as near to them as their dimensions would admit of; and his neck was usually garnished with a bright yellow handkerchief. In summer he carried in his mouth a flower; in winter, a straw – slight, but to a contemplative mind, certain indications of a love of nature, and a taste for botany.

• THROUGH A CHILD'S EYES •

Dickens had a peculiar talent for showing us the world using a child's perspective and privileging his or her point of view. In *Great Expectations*, Pip is subjected to what must be the most miserable Christmas dinner in the whole of English literature – a surprise perhaps, coming from the man who did so much to 'invent Christmas'. Pip does not merely suffer his own personal agonies over his still secret 'crime' (he has stolen some food), he is made a representative of an entire generation by adults complacently exercising their prejudices over food and wine:

It began the moment we sat down to dinner. Mr Wopsle said grace with a theatrical declamation …

and ended with the very proper aspiration that we might be truly grateful. Upon which my sister fixed me with her eye, and said, in a low reproachful voice, 'Do you hear that? Be grateful.'

'Especially,' said Mr Pumblechook, 'be grateful, boy, to them which brought you up by hand.'

Mrs. Hubble shook her head, and contemplating me with a mournful presentiment that I should come to no good, asked, 'Why is it that the young are never grateful?' This moral mystery seemed too much for the company until Mr. Hubble tersely solved it by saying, 'Naterally wicious.' Everybody then murmured 'True!' and looked at me in a particularly unpleasant and personal manner.

Paul Dombey is the son and heir of Mr Dombey, a great capitalist and businessman. Always sickly, he dies barely a quarter of the way through *Dombey and Son*. His final term at his Brighton boarding school, during which all the adults involved in his story become aware of the serious nature of his illness, is a tour de force in which Dickens gives full rein to his technique of representing the point of view of a child. This even extends to allowing the narrative to 'pass out' with Paul, so that the reader experiences the same breaks in consciousness as the boy. Unlike Pip, though, Paul is not telling his own story, so it is as if Paul takes over the novel and the narrator faints with him too:

> [There] … was no reason why he should be deaf, but he must have been, he thought, for, by and by, he heard Mr. Feeder calling in his ear, and gently shaking him to rouse his attention. And when he raised his head, quite scared, and looked about him, he found that Doctor Blimber had come into the room; and that the window was open, and that his forehead was wet with sprinkled water; though how all this had been done without his knowledge, was very curious indeed.

Paul is furthermore no respecter of persons, in the manner of a small child, and he is as interested in the man who comes to fix the clock as he is in the headmaster. The very building itself and its furniture is a friend to him and as real as the people within it. He wonders if the rooms will be lonely without his presence in them; he feels the portraits looking at him. It all makes for an otherworldly, disorientating narrative.

Dombey and Son was a great success and part V, describing Paul's illness and death, was a sensation. William Makepeace Thackeray was working for *Punch* at the time; he famously burst into the magazine's office and threw the number on the table, crying: 'There's no writing against such power as this – one has no chance! Read that chapter describing Paul's death: it is unsurpassed – it is stupendous.'

• IN THE MARGINS •

There is a famous letter by the writer Mary Russell Mitford about the public sensation caused by the early parts of *The Pickwick Papers*. Her correspondent, living in Ireland, is unaware of this latest literary phenomenon. Mitford explains: 'Well, they publish a number once a month and print 25,000 … It's fun – London life but without anything unpleasant; a lady might read it all *aloud* …'

Dickens remained proud of the 'safe' nature of his work – throughout his career he felt very deeply his responsibility to produce material that would not offend anyone (except the targets of his satire): writing that was 'family friendly'. What he never intended is that his work should be what we might call today 'middle of the road' or mainstream. In fact, compared to other great Victorian writers, he has a marked interest in extreme behaviour, and in minds and bodies that are out of the ordinary. Those whom others might marginalise appear in Dickens on the main stage.

One of the striking things about Dickens' work is his concern with bodies that do not fit a 'standard pattern'. We know that a human 'standard' is something of a fiction itself, but read any other famous Victorian novelist and you can see how normalising their fictional worlds are. In Dickens we meet a lot of people we might today call disabled.

This subject can be an uncomfortable one because of the way society and its language has changed. Dickens will write of 'cripples' and 'dwarves', and we might feel that sometimes he is using a character's appearance as a sign of their moral worth. But he was generally free of the more identifiable kinds of bigotry, or was willing to learn. He was persuaded, for instance, to change the character of Miss Mowcher in *David Copperfield*, after the woman who inspired her appearance contacted him and objected. In the end, she proves herself on the side of the angels by being responsible for the arrest of Steerforth's odious servant Littimer.

Making any modern diagnosis of fictional characters is silly really, but it is nevertheless interesting to note how wide ranging Dickens' presentation of 'disability' is. There is Jenny Wren (*Our Mutual Friend*), whose back is 'bad' and whose 'legs are queer'; Silas Wegg (*Our Mutual Friend*), who has a wooden leg; Bertha Plummer (*The Cricket on the Hearth*), who is blind; Miss Mowcher herself, who is a 'dwarf'; Wemmick's 'Aged P' (*Great Expectations*), who is deaf; Joe Willett (*Barnaby Rudge*), an amputee; Mrs Clennam (*Little Dorrit*), who uses a wheelchair; Captain Cuttle (*Dombey and Son*), who has one hand; Tiny Tim (*A Christmas Carol*), who 'bore a little crutch, and had his limbs supported by an iron frame'; and so on. This is just part of a cast list without parallel amongst Dickens' nineteenth-century colleagues. Why is he so different?

For a start, he sees more, or sees differently anyway. Dickens is an artist who relies on a strong and surprising depiction of the physical world to achieve his effects. His art needs variety. If other writers noticed these things, they bypassed them or even censored their own writing to remove them as (at best) distractions or (at worst) offensive. Dickens does also have his own peculiar take on the physical presence of human beings, and it is one of the things that keeps his writing fresh and keeps us on our toes as readers. He is especially fond of describing people as things, and things as people. Bentley Drummle, for instance, in *Great Expectations*, is 'an old-looking young man of a heavy order of architecture'. Miss Twinkleton's schoolhouse, on the other hand, in *The Mystery of Edwin Drood*, 'is so old and worn, and the brass plate is so shining and staring, that the general result has reminded imaginative strangers of a battered old beau with a large modern eye-glass stuck in his blind eye'.

It is therefore not surprising to discover that Dickens finds particularly fruitful the territory where people or parts of people *become* objects. He is fascinated by corpses, for example, and his visits to the Paris morgue became the occasion for one of his most compelling essays ('Some recollections of mortality' in *The Uncommercial Traveller*). And artificial aids such as crutches, hooks, sticks and wooden legs especially attract his attention. Indeed, Silas Wegg's missing limb is something of an ongoing theme in *Our Mutual Friend*. It interests Mr Boffin, who employs him, and is his principal reason for cultivating the acquaintance of Mr Venus, the bone articulator, since by this means he recovers his 'property' (his own leg – in 'a sort of brown paper truncheon'). When reading to Mr Boffin later about the lives of famous misers, his mind becomes so full of the thought of riches secretly concealed around him, that his artificial limb becomes as lively as flesh: '(Here Mr Wegg's wooden leg started forward under the table, and slowly elevated itself as he read on.)'

If we also take notice of minds and mental states in our search through the margins, we find that Dickens again is distinctive. Madness and badness can be found in other authors' work, but Dickens also includes figures such as Barnaby Rudge (whose 'pale face' was 'strangely lighted up by something that was not intellect') and Dr Manette from *A Tale of Two Cities*, whose mental collapse under imprisonment is shown by his compulsive devotion to making shoes. Addiction too, and its consequences, appears again and again throughout Dickens' work, especially in the form of alcoholism; for every figure of fun like Rev. Stiggins, there is a Mr Wickfield (*David Copperfield*) or a Mr Dolls (*Our Mutual Friend*) or a Krook (*Bleak House*) – or a Jasper, whose opium-induced vision provides such a disorientating beginning to *The Mystery of Edwin Drood.*

• EATING •

For Dickens, eating and drinking was at the heart of human relations. Sharing the Christmas pudding is an activity that binds the Cratchits together in *A Christmas Carol*. It is how they know who they are.

Throughout Dickens' books, people get together over food at parties, at balls, at funerals and in taverns, in restaurants and in the workhouse. They eat on the move, in stagecoaches and steamboats; they eat to settle themselves at home. Dickens also uses food to prompt our compassion, from the 'dreary waste of cold potatoes, looking as eatable as Stonehenge' that are offered to the 'small servant' in *The Old Curiosity Shop* to the more political description of the workhouse diet in *Oliver Twist*:

> [The Board] established the rule, that all poor people should have the alternative … of being starved by a gradual process in the workhouse, or by a quick one out of it. With this view, they contracted with the water-works to lay on an unlimited supply of water; and with a corn-factor to supply periodically small quantities of oatmeal; and issued three meals of thin gruel a day, with an onion twice a week, and half a roll on Sundays.

Reading Dickens, we become familiar not just with the densely detailed language associated with Victorian food, like the 'particular style of loaf' in *Martin Chuzzlewit*, 'which is known to housekeepers as a slack-baked, crummy quartern' but also with the special behaviours inseparable from eating and drinking. We might be after a chop along with the young men of *Bleak House*:

Quickly the waitress returns, bearing what is apparently a model of the tower of Babel, but what is really a pile of plates and flat tin dish-covers ... Then, amidst a constant coming in, and going out, and running about, and a clatter of crockery, and a rumbling up and down of the machine which brings the nice cuts from the kitchen, and a shrill crying for more nice cuts down the speaking pipe ... [they] appease their appetites.

Or we might observe the elaborate rituals of the dinner parties in *Our Mutual Friend*; young bachelors in lodgings sending out for meals (and servants to attend them) like David Copperfield; or the practice of working-class people cooking away from home, because, used to merely warming things over an open fire, they do not possess such a thing as an oven:

The bakers' shops in the humbler suburbs ... are filled with men, women, and children, each anxiously waiting for the Sunday dinner. Look at the group of children who surround that working man who has just emerged from the baker's shop at the corner of the street, with the reeking dish, in which a diminutive joint of mutton simmers above a vast heap of half-browned potatoes.

All of this is, of course, fertile ground for social comment, as Sam Weller reminds us in his inimitable way. Oysters, far from being the delicacy they are considered today, were a cheap working-class staple in the nineteenth century:

'It's a wery remarkable circumstance, Sir,' said Sam, 'that poverty and oysters always seem to go together.'

'I don't understand you, Sam,' said Mr. Pickwick.

'What I mean, sir,' said Sam, 'is, that the poorer a place is, the greater call there seems to be for oysters. Look here, sir; here's a oyster-stall to every half-dozen houses. The street's lined with 'em. Blessed if I don't think that ven a man's wery poor, he rushes out of his lodgings, and eats oysters in reg'lar desperation.'

The seal of the Rochester Oyster and Floating Fishery, used at its 'Admiralty Court' to administer the profitable Victorian Medway oyster grounds. (With the permission of the Guildhall Museum)

• DRINKING •

Dickens was aware of the dangers of heavy drinking, but was not sympathetic to those who suggested that everyone should give up all alcohol. He sees the context. In writing about 'Gin Shops' in *Sketches by Boz*, he notices how pubs use bright lights and fancy designs to tempt people inside, especially people whose homes were perhaps poor, dirty and dull. The gin shop in the middle of the street, with 'the illuminated clock, the plate-glass windows … and its profusion of gas-lights in richly-gilt burners, is perfectly dazzling when contrasted with the darkness and dirt' of the rest of the neighbourhood. But he thinks the problem lies with the dirt, not with the drinking: 'Gin-drinking is a great vice in England, but wretchedness and dirt are a

> *By Dickens' time gin was already thought of as* **the** **drink that brought ruin on the working classes. But** *'gin' was often simply a catch-all name that covered a multitude of evils – grain spirit 'enhanced' with additions of minimal flavour and varying toxicity. Unregulated variety was the norm. In Dickens, the drink is often made to order and to an individual recipe. Each glass or tumbler or bowl can be different.*

greater; and until you improve the homes of the poor ... gin-shops will increase in number and splendour.'

Pubs had reputations to preserve, for mixing good-quality drinks to reliable recipes, as well as for buying from reputable suppliers. The Six Jolly Fellowship Porters in *Our Mutual Friend* advertises itself as 'The Early Purl House' to encourage perhaps those very porters to look in for liquid sustenance and encouragement before tackling the day's work. It is a 'speciality' of the house. Heated alcoholic drinks were in demand in the morning for the large number of people working outside – as they were at the other end of the day for those retiring to sleep in unheated bedrooms.

These drinks demanded special equipment. In a pub, there was always likely to be a fire nearby, of course. Customers in the Six Jolly Fellowship Porters 'were provided with comfortable fireside tin utensils, like models of sugar-loaf hats, made in that shape that they might, with their pointed ends, seek out for themselves glowing nooks in the depths of the red coals, when they mulled your ale ...'

WHAT'LL YOU HAVE?

PURL

Purl is dark beer, heated and spiced, and fortified with gin. It has a good, long London history and enjoys immortal fame for its role in bringing together Dick Swiveller and the Marchioness in *The Old Curiosity Shop*:

'There!' said Richard, putting the plate before her. 'First of all clear that off, and then you'll see what's next.'

The small servant needed no second bidding, and the plate was soon empty.

'Next,' said Dick, handing the purl, 'take a pull at that; but moderate your transports, you know, for you're not used to it. Well, is it good?'

'Oh! Isn't it?' said the small servant.

FLIP

Flip could be made of wine or beer, and it could be taken hot or cold, but the one invariable appears to have been egg whisked in. It was thought of as a 'stiffener' or pick-me-up, and indeed it is the drink that Dickens himself used to fortify his nerves during his public readings. Many pubs kept a 'flip dog' by the fire along with the other hearth-side utensils; this could be heated and plunged into the drink to warm it: 'Mrs. Chickenstalker's notion of a little flip did honour to her character. The pitcher steamed and smoked and reeked like a volcano; and the man who had carried it, was faint.'

DOG'S NOSE

This is little more than a rough purl, thrown together at speed. The Wellers, father and son, attend a temperance meeting in the *The Pickwick Papers* where reports are read out giving the public the testimony of recent converts to the cause:

H. Walker, tailor, wife, and two children. When in better circumstances, owns to having been in the constant habit of drinking ale and beer; says he is not certain whether he did not twice a week, for twenty years, taste 'dog's nose', which your committee find upon inquiry, to be compounded of warm porter, moist sugar, gin, and nutmeg (a groan, and 'So it is!' from an elderly female). Is now out of work and penniless; thinks it must be the porter (cheers) or the loss of the use of his right hand; is not certain which, but thinks it very likely that, if he had drunk nothing but water all his life, his fellow workman would never have stuck a rusty needle in him, and thereby occasioned his accident (tremendous cheering). Has nothing but cold water to drink, and never feels thirsty (great applause).

BISHOP

Another drink made famous by Dickens. Bishop resembles the mulled wine that many people like to make today in winter. It came in various types, each of which would be identified by the clerical rank used to describe it. Bishop is made with port. It is bishop that cements the renewed relationship between Scrooge (who has learned his lesson) and his clerk Bob Cratchit (who can hardly believe his ears):

'A merry Christmas, Bob,' said Scrooge, with an earnestness that could not be mistaken, as he clapped him on the back. 'A merrier Christmas, Bob, my good fellow, than I have given you for many a year. I'll raise your salary, and endeavour to assist your struggling family, and we will discuss your affairs this very afternoon, over a Christmas bowl of smoking bishop, Bob.'

A china cup complete with a printed image of Rochester and its 'new bridge'. This was opened in 1856, the year Dickens bought Gad's Hill Place. (With the permission of the Guildhall Museum)

PUNCH

Finally: a bowl of punch. Taken hot or cold and made with all kinds of spirits – plus citrus, sugar and sometimes spices – punch was made for sharing. It went down easily:

This constant succession of glasses produced considerable effect upon Mr. Pickwick; his countenance beamed with the most sunny smiles, laughter played around his lips, and good-humoured merriment twinkled in his eye. Yielding by degrees to the influence of the exciting liquid, rendered more so by the heat, Mr. Pickwick expressed a strong desire to recollect a song which he had heard in his infancy, and the attempt proving abortive, sought to stimulate his memory with more glasses of punch, which appeared to have quite a contrary effect; for, from forgetting the words of the song, he began to forget how to articulate any words at all; and finally, after rising to his legs to address the company in an eloquent speech, he fell into the barrow, and fast asleep, simultaneously.

PART 3

READING

· 10 ·

THE STORYTELLER

What makes reading Dickens different?

The first thing to say is that Dickens is a very uneven writer. His prose seems to jump about and change its tone, its point of view, even who seems to be speaking. Sometimes this seems intrusive; sometimes it is merely bewildering. He repeats himself. He seems to be shouting at someone. He writes sentences that seem to go round and about. Then he writes some that don't seem to have enough words in. He notices his characters, and will sometimes tell us things about them that they appear to contradict.

All of this makes Dickens sound like a character in one of his own novels, which of course he is. In fact, perhaps he is *the* character in his own novels. We have a relationship with Dickens that is not like that which we have with other writers. At least he thought so. He

asked John Forster, when he was attempting to justify
the paid readings he gave in the later part of his life, to
consider the impact on his readership – 'that particular relation (personally affectionate and like no other
man's) which subsists between me and the public ...'

Just look at a few beginnings. There is *Bleak House*:

> London. Michaelmas term lately over, and the Lord
> Chancellor sitting in Lincoln's Inn Hall. Implacable
> November weather ...
>
> Fog everywhere. Fog up the river, where it flows
> among green aits and meadows; fog down the river,
> where it rolls deified among the tiers of shipping and
> the waterside pollutions of a great (and dirty) city.
> Fog on the Essex marshes, fog on the Kentish heights.

All these sentences, stacked one upon the other,
come up as 'fragments' in any spellchecker because
they don't have main verbs. They pose at being 'mere'
statements, run into a list.

There is *Little Dorrit*:

> Everything in Marseilles, and about Marseilles, had
> stared at the fervid sky, and been stared at in return,
> until a staring habit had become universal there.
> Strangers were stared out of countenance by star-

ing white houses, staring white walls, staring white streets, staring tracts of arid road, staring hills from which verdure was burnt away. The only things to be seen not fixedly staring and glaring were the vines drooping under their load of grapes.

And the staring continues as we turn the page and read through the first chapter. The word 'stare' ends up staring at us out of the page. Although Dickens is interested in the physical world, and wants us to be interested in the physical world, often what we notice first is Dickens. The arresting way he serves it all up brings him to our attention. He does not retreat behind the picture, but stands in front of it and points out what we should find interesting.

And, of course, there is *A Christmas Carol*:

Marley was dead. To begin with. There is no doubt whatever about that.

Startlingly direct, but playful, with its pose of seeming very certain about something that is clearly going to be completely out of the ordinary, the narrator here seems to have grabbed us by the arm and begun almost in a spirit of contradiction as if we were daring to express any doubt ourselves. How different from the other two beginnings we have seen! But, at the same time, how much a part of the Dickens voice, or voices.

Those voices are so numerous as to be almost unnameable, although there are a few with which the Dickens reader becomes familiar before very long. There is the speechifying rhetoric that tends to burst out in defence of the oppressed. Over the death of Jo, for instance, in *Bleak House*:

Dead, your Majesty. Dead my lords and gentlemen. Dead, Right Reverends and Wrong Reverends of every order. Dead, men and women, born with heavenly compassion in your hearts. And dying thus around us, every day.

Or over Betty Higden in *Our Mutual Friend*, who would rather die than go into the workhouse:

A surprising spirit in this lonely woman after so many years of hard working and hard living, my Lords and Gentlemen and Honourable Boards!

There is the rather gross approval of the indulgent author towards his favoured creations – an author who is determined that we should not marshal our own sympathies but be dragooned into compliance, such as over Ruth Pinch's apron:

> She didn't put it on up stairs, but came dancing down with it in her hand; and being one of those little women to whom an apron is a most becoming little vanity, it took an immense time to arrange; having to be carefully smoothed down beneath – Oh heaven, what a wicked little stomacher! – and to be gathered up into little plaits by the strings before it could be tied …

Or Mrs Peerybingle in *The Cricket on the Hearth*, who looks out of a darkened window and sees her own reflection:

> And my opinion is (and so would yours have been), that she might have looked a long way, and seen nothing half so agreeable.

And finally there is the tone Dickens adopts which is that of a man who has found out the world and needs to explain to us how it is:

> You couldn't walk about in Todgers's neighbourhood, as you could in any other neighbourhood. You groped your way for about an hour though lanes and

bye-ways, and courtyards and passages; and never once emerged upon anything that might reasonably be called a street.

This is posing as something beyond fiction, as *living*, and it is the backdrop to what is going to become the narrative, which in turn finds itself embedded in a world of habitual activity that we now find we share. It can be general:

> There are very few moments in a man's existence, when he experiences so much ludicrous distress, or meets with so little charitable commiseration, as when he is in pursuit of his own hat.

It can be decidedly specific:

> Whosoever had gone out of Fleet Street into the Temple at the date of this history, and had wandered disconsolate about the Temple until he stumbled on a dismal churchyard, and had looked up at the dismal windows commanding that churchyard until at the most dismal window of them all he saw a dismal boy …

It is Dickens preparing the ground – or more properly the stage – on which he is to perform, and which he wants the reader to recognise, so that he or she can do the work necessary to bring the events of the book to life. When Dickens was, in later life, actually performing with his real voice on a real platform, he noted these efforts people made to make his work live. He wrote to Forster: 'The affectionate regard of the people exceeds all bounds and is shown in every way. The audiences do everything but embrace me, and take as much pains with the readings as I do.'

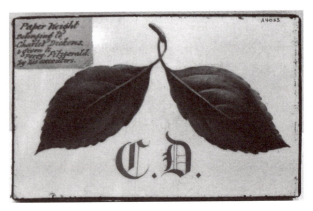

Dickens' paperweight, given to him by Shakespeare scholar Mary Cowden Clarke. 'I have a reminder of you always before me,' he wrote to her. 'On my desk stand two green leaves, which I every morning station in their evergreen place at my elbow.' (The Percy Fitzgerald collection, with the permission of the Guildhall Museum)

11

A READER'S WORK

· LOOKING ·

WHAT IS THE WORK the reader has to do when picking up a Dickens novel? The book we sit with today is often not the same as its Victorian ancestor. We do not read Dickens in the way his own contemporaries read him. To begin with, it might be worth bearing in mind the impact of the original format of his work; revolutionary as it was, it has now been largely superseded. One of the important features of this format, which we all too often forget, was illustration.

When Dickens came to write a preface for the 1847 cheap edition of the spectacularly successful *The Pickwick Papers*, and to describe the novel's genesis, he was in no doubt as to the value of the contribution his illustrator had made:

I thought of Mr Pickwick and wrote the first number; from the proof sheets of which, MR SEYMOUR made his drawing of the Club, and that happy portrait of its founder, by which he is always recognised, and which may be said to have made him a reality.

In some ways, these are amazing things for a writer of Dickens' stature and nature to concede: he thought of Mr Pickwick, of course, but Seymour made him a reality. There could hardly be a better indication of the importance of the role of the illustrator in Dickens' own eyes.

Of the novels, only *Hard Times* and *Great Expectations* appeared without pictures. Furthermore, such was the pressure of each deadline that Dickens' collaborating artists had to work from notes and hints from the author when he had hardly sat down to work. They sketched a design and had it approved, in many cases before the text was complete. So Dickens' novel illustrations are full of inconsistencies where the artist has guessed at details that, in the event, did not turn up in the narrative. They are an interpretation of his first thoughts and inspirations. And the greatest of them are intensely sympathetic to the action, with its many perspectives, dense physical context and pervasive atmosphere.

So what could those original readers expect for their money?

For the novels in monthly parts, first came a cover. Or, more correctly, a coloured paper wrapper that included front, back and spine. On this, of course, was printed the title, author and so on, but also a 'teaser' design which related to the book's content. This was tricky to get right, because it did not change throughout the life of the nineteen issues that contained the twenty parts. For *Oliver Twist* there was no problem, because it had already been published in magazine form before it got a wrapper, but for many of the other novels the design needed to attract the reader without giving the story away. Cleverly, Hablot Browne adopted the motif of a 'progress' or 'wheel of fortune', which led figures in a rise and fall up and down the cover. In this way he was able to use exemplary and non-specific detail to suggest the context and general drift of the narrative without including identifiable characters (although some were representative).

Inside the cover were advertisements, then two pictures. These were printed on good-quality paper and bound into the part in front of the text. Sometimes booksellers extracted them and displayed them in their windows to tempt passers-by to purchase the latest instalment. So Dickens' illustrators came to expect their plates to be linked rather more strongly with each other than with the printed word itself. They were paired, and not dropped into the narrative in the way we might expect today.

The last part of the monthly series was a double and contained four pictures. There were the usual two derived from the narrative, then a frontispiece and a title page, complete with small illustration. The purchaser could then bind the entire collection of parts, placing these two final plates facing each other at the beginning of the volume. For *Nicholas Nickleby*, the reader got a portrait of the author on the frontispiece, now fully acknowledging himself as serious artist 'Charles Dickens' rather than the matey 'Boz'. But later Hablot Browne made the most of the pairing within the bound volume to design images that complimented each other: in *Little Dorrit*, for example, he depicts Amy entering the Merdle household with her sister on the frontispiece, as she leaves the Marshalsea prison (bound opposite) in a raking shaft of light.

There were variations on this formula. In *The Old Curiosity Shop and Barnaby Rudge*, which appeared in Dickens' magazine *Master Humphrey's Clock*, the pictures are set into the text. *A Tale of Two Cities* was published weekly (without illustrations) and then slightly later in eight monthly parts with illustrations by Browne. The Christmas Books were lavish productions, with many artists involved. *A Christmas Carol* itself even contained four pictures with full hand colouring.

• LAUGHING •

During his lifetime, Dickens was mainly thought of as a comic writer. People also found him very funny, which is not always the same thing. We see the comic Dickens in his happy endings, but also the licence he is able to take with violence (*The Pickwick Papers*) and his fondness for stereotypes. To make us laugh, Dickens strove to choose the right words. His attachment to words can betray him into an obsession with thinking that some words (especially long ones) are funnier than they really are or that some get funnier the more they are used, which is occasionally, though rarely, the case. Dickens plays with words as a kind of default mode, a way of establishing a kind of tone, and it is not always conspicuously successful; but it is part of who he is. So when he says Mr Stiggins, 'staggering to and fro in the excitement of his eloquence, was fain to catch at the back of a chair to preserve his perpendicular', he is playing a game of pretending to avert his eyes from the behaviour of one of his characters. The long formal words cover up (very poorly) the fact that Stiggins is falling-over drunk.

In *Great Expectations*, when Pip and Herbert visit the chaotic Pocket household, the children are brought into the adults after dinner. Silly Mrs Pocket is rather at a loss, having her mind on other things:

> 'Here! Give me your fork, Mum, and take the baby,' said Flopson. 'Don't take it that way, or you'll get its head under the table.'
>
> Thus advised, Mrs. Pocket took it the other way, and got its head upon the table; which was announced to all present by a prodigious concussion.

Here Dickens is able to avoid actually mentioning the plain reality of what happens: the baby bangs its head. It is passed over, like the drunkenness of Stiggins. Dickens imitates the phrase of one of his own characters (Flopson, the maid) instead: Mrs Pocket 'got its head upon the table'. Then he can use the absurd 'announced' and the wonderful 'prodigious', coupled with the vaguely scientific 'concussion', as if the baby has done something remarkable.

There are also funny situations, as well as funny words. Set-piece comedy was a staple of the plays and novels of Dickens' childhood. The adult Dickens rolls these out with gusto. He was well placed to do so, having a quick eye both for the conventions of works of art and the corporate follies of groups (or types) of people. His handling of what we would call stereotypes shows how surefooted he is in this area, and how his skill elevates the cheapest of materials into something enduring and even magical.

The Pickwick Papers, for instance, is about stereotypes. Everybody in 1836 agreed that was the plan. Even its situations are stereotypical: the novel opens with a tedious society meeting about nothing that would have been readily identifiable among its audience. And, in fact, the case of mistaken identity that leads to a duel for poor Mr Winkle is lifted directly from eighteenth-century novelist Tobias Smollett.

It is all very knowing. Dickens even inserts a character (Mr Jingle) who appears to be as aware as Dickens of the conventions on display. Or as aware as us perhaps, since he reads the Pickwickians like a book. Spotting the poet in Mr Snodgrass, he spins a preposterous tale about writing an 'Epic poem, – ten thousand lines' during the 1830 July Revolution ('fired a musket, – fired with an idea' etc.). Turning to Winkle, he claims ownership of a 'sagacious' dog that would not enter an enclosure one day and was found staring at a sign that said 'Gamekeeper has orders to shoot all dogs found in this enclosure'. And 'Fine girl, sir', he says to the susceptible Mr Tupman.

The book is full of this kind of thing (Mr Pickwick chasing his hat; Mr Pickwick in a lady's bedroom; Mr Pickwick tricked into breaking into a girls' school) but what stops it being tedious, and what perhaps points towards Dickens' increasingly sophisticated handling of distinctiveness, individuality and the familiar in his later career, is the way he gives it his all. It is as though someone forgot to tell the Pickwickians that they are only puppets in a farce.

They claim a kind of dignity that seems impervious to our assessment of whether they are dignified or not. It is the claim that is important, not the dignity. People remember Bill Sikes and Mr Micawber and what they are like when their recall of the characters' actual stories is patchy. In fact, in remembering character in this way, we have already separated them from their stories – we remember who they are, rather than what they do. Mrs Gamp, as a hired nurse, is part of the plot of *Martin Chuzzlewit* and she also belongs in an identifiable line of incompetent medical stereotypes, but neither seems important when we can luxuriate in writing like this:

The face of Mrs Gamp – the nose in particular – was somewhat red and swollen, and it was difficult to enjoy her society without becoming conscious of a smell of spirits. Like most persons who have attained to great eminence in their profession, she took to hers very kindly; insomuch that, setting aside her natural predilections as a woman, she went to a lying-in or a laying-out with equal zest and relish.

'Ah!' repeated Mrs Gamp; for it was always a safe sentiment in cases of mourning. 'Ah dear! When Gamp was summoned to his long home, and I see him a-lying in Guy's Hospital with a penny-piece on each eye, and his wooden leg under his left arm, I thought I should have fainted away. But I bore up ...'

'You have become indifferent since then, I suppose?' said Mr Pecksniff. 'Use is second nature, Mrs Gamp.'

'You may well say second nater, sir,' returned that lady. 'One's first ways is to find sich things a trial to the feelings, and so is one's lasting custom. If it wasn't for the nerve a little sip of liquor gives me (I never was able to do more than taste it), I never could go through with what I sometimes has to do. "Mrs Harris," I says, at the very last case as ever I acted in, which it was but a young person, "Mrs Harris," I says, "leave the bottle on the chimley-piece, and don't ask me to take none, but let me put my lips to it when I am so dispoged, and then I will do what I'm engaged to do, according to the best of my ability." "Mrs Gamp," she says, in answer, "if ever there was a sober creetur to be got at eighteen pence a day for working people, and three and six for gentlefolks – night watching,'" said Mrs Gamp with emphasis, '"being a extra charge – you are that inwallable person." "Mrs Harris," I says to her, "don't name the charge, for if I could afford to lay all my feller creeturs out for nothink, I would gladly do it, sich is the love I bears 'em. But what I always says to them as has the management of matters, Mrs Harris'" – here she kept her eye on Mr Pecksniff – '"be they gents or be they ladies, is, don't ask me whether I won't take none, or whether I will, but leave the bottle on the chimley-piece, and let me put my lips to it when I am so dispoged."'

Here Dickens does not pretend to avert his eyes, as with Stiggins. In fact, he gives us the inside line as to what Mrs Gamp is really like. He tells us she is always drunk and hints at her mercenary nature. But none of this matters. Mrs Gamp is a 'comic' character, but she is much more than merely funny. She is astonishingly alive. Somehow Dickens per-

The incomparable Mrs Gamp, in Ivorex. (With the permission of
the Guildhall Museum)

suades us to accept her eccentricity as evidence of her existence, rather than allowing us to refuse it as an absurdity. So the spectacle of Mr Gamp, with his wooden leg under his left arm, the bottle on the 'chimley-piece', the fictitious Mrs Harris and the mangled language, are individually delightful but also part of an integrated richness. When Mrs Gamp hands over her card and says, 'Gamp is my name and Gamp my nater', we can only agree that it is ridiculously, magnificently, true.

• CRYING •

We have somehow forgotten how emotional the Victorians could be. The 'buttoned-up' stereotype misses the public displays of feeling people were used to within families, amongst friends and at communal events. Dickens himself, when he finished his second Christmas Book, *The Chimes*, celebrated with 'a real good cry'. He rushed back to England from Genoa to read it to a group of friends, including Daniel Maclise, who reported 'shrieks of laughter … floods of tears' amongst the assembled company. Indeed, as he reflected on this reading and wrote to his wife about it, Dickens showed that he valued these tokens of emotion enormously: 'If you could have seen Macready last night – undisguisedly sobbing, and crying on the sofa, as I read – you would have felt (as I did) what a thing it is to have Power.'

Especially early in his career, Dickens wrote to generate intense emotional response, and the deaths of Nell in *The Old Curiosity Shop* and Paul in *Dombey and Son* became famous, and then notorious, examples of his pursuit of this effect. Lord Jeffrey, founder and editor of the *Edinburgh Review*, wrote after reading of the death of Paul:

> Oh, my dear, dear Dickens! What a No. 5 you have given us! I have so cried and sobbed over it last night, and again this morning; and felt my heart so purified by those tears, and blessed and loved you for making me shed them …

Fashion (and Dickens' art) had begun to change before his death in 1870, and although we still find ourselves at the bedside of dying children, there is not the same massaging of effect that we experience above all in *The Old Curiosity Shop*, where, although Little Nell dies off page, her body is lingeringly exhibited to draw forth grief:

For she was dead. There, upon her little bed, she lay at rest. The solemn stillness was no marvel now.

She was dead. No sleep so beautiful and calm, so free from trace of pain, so fair to look upon. She seemed a creature fresh from the hand of God, and waiting for the breath of life; not one who had lived and suffered death.

Her couch was dressed with here and there some winter berries and green leaves, gathered in a spot she had been used to favour. 'When I die, put near me something that has loved the light, and had the sky above it always.' Those were her words.

She was dead. Dear, gentle, patient, noble Nell was dead. Her little bird – a poor slight thing the pressure of a finger would have crushed – was stirring nimbly in its cage; and the strong heart of its child mistress was mute and motionless for ever.

Dickens is cranking the machinery here for all he is worth. The repetition, the 'fake' straightforwardness ('She was dead'), the presentation of the death as a spectacle ('There, upon her little bed …'; 'Those were her words'), the bird, the uncorrupted corpse – it's all in there. Dickens keeps the ugly business of dying itself from us – and from Nell – so that we can more comfortably adore the body.

Compare this with Dickens' last completed novel, *Our Mutual Friend*. The boy Johnny dies while we are watching, and although Dickens acts upon our feelings by having him give away all his toys and pass on a kiss in his precocious awareness of impending oblivion, his final moments are artistically rigorously controlled:

> With a weary and yet a pleased smile, and with an action as if he stretched his little figure out to rest, the child heaved his body on the sustaining arm, and seeking Rokesmith's face with his lips, said:
>
> 'A kiss for the boofer lady.'
>
> Having now bequeathed all he had to dispose of, and arranged his affairs in this world, Johnny, thus speaking, left it.

• PERFORMING •

Is there such as thing as 'a Dickens reader'? Or are there just people who read Dickens? The advantage of looking at Dickens' readership in particular is that its activities have been peculiarly well documented for more than a hundred years in *The Dickensian*, the journal of The Dickens Fellowship.

The fellowship was founded in London in 1902. Its objectives are interesting. They include a desire 'to knit together in a common bond of friendship lovers of the great master of humour and pathos, Charles Dickens', to campaign against those social evils that he especially abhorred and 'to assist in the preservation and purchase of buildings and objects associated with his name or mentioned in his works'. In particular, the link between the work and the world (those 'buildings and objects' and their importance) might give us a clue as to how distinctive Dickens readers might be. These objectives are themselves a record of

The Rochester Guildhall or 'the Town Hall near at hand' of *Great Expectations*, where Pip is formally apprenticed to Joe. (With the permission of the Guildhall Museum)

a Dickens legacy, which was itself growing into something of a programme during the later years of the nineteenth century. As Dickens noted of the audience at his public readings, this programme is strenuously creative: Dickens readers 'take … pains' and they are active – they get out into the world.

• SPACES & PLACES •

A number of 'Dickensian' books were published between Dickens' death in 1870 and the start of the fellowship. These attempted in various ways to define a geography of Dickens' fiction: to find the place where it all happened. This was an extensive process, and it is still going on. It involves a substantial knowledge of Dickens' biography, complete familiarity with his work and considerable critical skills, a detailed awareness of the physical shape of the real landscape in question and unbounded energy to rival Dickens' own. As well as, of course, being gloriously impossible. Enough attempts in print had already been made for Robert Langton to refer to them rather tartly in an edition of his *Childhood and Youth of Charles Dickens*, published in 1891. This was an important book that aimed at an expansion of the details in Forster's early biography and was itself part of a growing interest in the years in Kent that were such a significant feature of either end of Dickens' life.

So the Dickens country that began to take shape at about this time looked a lot like Kent. When William Hughes wrote *A Week's Tramp in Dickens-Land*, describing a walking tour he made in 1888, beating the bounds of this country becoming known as peculiarly Dickens', he relegated London to what he called a 'preliminary tramp' only and made his headquarters 'at Rochester'. Turn-of-the-century London was becoming rather thin pickings for those interested in the coaching days of the classic Dickens novel or sketch. *A Week's Tramp* was, in the main, 'the record of a pilgrimage' and, in the fashion of pilgrims, Hughes and his friend Frederick Kitton go partly to confirm their faith in the reality of what they believe; one of their aims is 'to go over and verify some of the most important localities rendered famous in the novels'.

This impulse towards verification is a noticeable trait of Dickensian activity and it is the secret itch of the Dickens reader. We are seduced by the peculiar persuasiveness of the Dickens world. We know from Mamie's account of Dickens working, and from his own description of London as his 'magic lantern', that there seems to have been a way in which Dickens first

performed his work (just in his head, perhaps), looked
at it and wrote it down. This comes through when we
meet characters like Mrs Gamp or Mr Micawber: their
self-contained, self-assertive identity seems independent of anything but themselves. Our natural reaction
is to wonder what or who Dickens was watching when
he gathered these details for our enjoyment. It seems
the least likely thing of all that he should just have
made them up. Thus a popular Dickensian pastime for
more than a hundred years has been to search for the
'originals' of these wonderful figures.

And, even more powerfully perhaps, the Dickens
reader cannot let go. What agony to close the book and
look up! Inside, it all feels as real as dinner: it must be
out there somewhere – to be touched, heard or walked
through. It is as if we have confused our memory of
reading with our memory of living. As William Hughes
says, walking down Rochester High Street:

> The air is full of Dickens. At every corner, and almost
> at the door of every house, we half expect to be met
> by one or other of the characters who will claim
> acquaintance with us as their friends or admirers.

Hughes' real experience of Rochester is being
transformed by these literary hallucinations. He re-

imagines the city's past to make it fall in line with his own past reading.

And it works the other way too: when the two pilgrims reach Eastgate House on the High Street, having enjoyed its full value as the 'original' of the girls' school in *The Mystery of Edwin Drood*, they make it fit another establishment in another novel: 'We feel morally certain that Eastgate House is also the prototype of Westgate House in the Pickwick Papers, although for the purposes of the story, it is therein located at Bury St Edmunds.'

Here is Hughes 'taking … pains' in the manner Dickens had observed, creatively re-imagining his reading to fit what he sees, as he has already re-imagined what he sees to fit his reading.

No wonder the language of history gets mixed up in all this. If Mr Pickwick and the rest are real enough to claim our acquaintance, they are certainly real enough to make the small sidestep out of fiction and into the past. Hughes tries to put his finger on it. He suggests it is all about technique. Each place Dickens describes may be 'previously known to us', 'but the fidelity of his descriptions and the reality of the characters peopling it, certainly give a historical value never before understood or appreciated'.

Somehow what was not accessible to us from the mere face of the world becomes part of what there was (in the form of the past) and is (in the form of history) because we read it in Dickens. We cannot believe what is true until it is made up. We cannot see what is really there until it is obscured by the imagination.

A Week's Tramp is quite a performance. Our two pilgrims are in no doubt about the precedence that Dickens' work takes over what they actually see in front of them. An inconclusive trip to Aylesford reveals that the physical details of the landscape refuse to conform to the fictional account preserved in *The Pickwick Papers*. So Hughes and Kitton 'console' themselves by reading the book and decide to 'make believe' that they have 'actually seen' Manor Farm, Dingley Dell. This imagining of fact is very different from the reading of fiction – a story that is to be enjoyed as an open expression of the imagination, whose truth is irrelevant. Instead, they are covering an emptiness (not finding the 'real' Dingley Dell) with a true lie, whose entire worth rests on the fact that they must believe it. Remember the preface to the cheap edition of *The Pickwick Papers*: Dickens, normally so jealous of his achievements, was surprisingly relaxed there about the business of making things real, handing the credit to his illustrator Robert Seymour. Perhaps this was because he did not see 'making things a reality' as his business. That was all down to his readers, and his readers' work. It is work we all do, but some readers leave a legacy of their own.

• FILM •

Dickens invented film. Or, perhaps more exactly, Film. At least, he did according to Sergei Eisenstein, the pioneering Soviet director, who made the magnificent silent film *Battleship Potemkin* in 1925. Eisenstein was conscious of how young the movie industry was and how immature it might seem as an art form. He wanted to establish a cultural heritage of film that would link it to the great works of art of the past. He began with D. W. Griffith, the director who did more than any other filmmaker to establish the visual language of the contemporary movie. This led quickly to Dickens. Griffith's wife, Linda Arvidson, remembered that he got into trouble with his studio for tying disparate scenes together and cutting quickly from one scenario to another. She claimed in her book, *When the Movies Were Young* (1925), that executives protested at the apparent incoherence:

'How can you tell a story jumping about like that? The people won't know what it's about.'

'Well,' said Mr Griffith, 'doesn't Dickens write that way?'

'Yes, but that's Dickens; that's novel writing; that's different.'

'Oh, not so much, these are picture stories; not so different.'

Griffith realised that the audience watching a film would be as creative as the readers of a novel in assembling their own coherent narrative from the dispersed events of a visual experience. In other words, he knew the sense of a film lay in the work of those watching it. This idea was picked up by Eisenstein, who identified how the heritage of filmmaking led back to Dickens and his narrative technique. He was particularly interested in a passage in *Oliver Twist*, in which Dickens discussed his presentation of the unfolding story:

It is the custom on the stage, in all good murderous melodramas, to present the tragic and the comic scenes, in as regular alternation, as the layers of red and white in a side of streaky bacon. The hero sinks upon his straw bed, weighed down by fetters and misfortunes; in the next scene, his faithful but unconscious squire regales the audience with a comic song ...

Such changes appear absurd; but they are not so unnatural as they appear at first sight. The transitions in real life from well-spread boards to death-beds, and from mourning weeds to holidays garments, are not a whit less startling; only, there, we are busy actors, instead of passive lookers-on; which makes a vast difference.

Eisenstein called this cutting-away technique 'montage'. Its identification was a major step in the growth of the possibilities of film – beyond the mere recording and dissemination of traditionally stage-bound productions. It may also lie behind Dickens' extraordinarily influential presence on screen.

With so many of Dickens' books being made into film, there is no question that today a huge audience knows their Dickens not from the printed page but from the silver screen (or the small one). This, in turn, has had an effect on Dickens' reputation as

Dickens' work has been adapted for film more often than that of any other author. Over eighty films have been produced since the first, in the 1890s, which was based on episodes from **Oliver Twist**. *All the novels have been filmed at least once.*

a representative 'great artist' and on his presence in our cultural life. In fact, the famous film adaptations of two works, *A Christmas Carol* and *Oliver Twist*, have become so popular that they have gone a long way towards elevating their status into myth – just 'stuff that we know about': bigger and more shadowy than the story told by the words on the page.

Watching Dickens films shows us how his work is still growing; in fact, Dickens himself was never really in control of it. We know that versions of *Oliver Twist* were appearing on the London stage before Dickens had got anywhere close to finishing the novel; the idea had got away from him and was living an independent life whether he cared or not. He could no longer own it. With this in mind, the liberties taken with the book by a phenomenon such as the *Oliver!* musical and its Carol Reed film version seem less surprising. Here, Fagin and the Dodger are allowed to escape and the atmosphere seems more naughty than Newgate.

12

DICKENS THE READER

IN THE 1850s, DICKENS took to the stage and embarked on what was to be an illustrious second career – paid public readings of his work. This was not quite unprecedented: it was possible to go and hear lectures by established writers and famous actors often gave recitals of popular works, especially Shakespeare. Bringing the two together, as Dickens did when he read his own work, was new. Even then, Dickens had been used to reading to audiences for a number of years in a private context (as we have seen, gleefully upsetting his friends with the stronger portions of *The Chimes*) and he had been quite willing to give charitable public readings for nothing. In 1858 he decided (against John Forster's advice, who argued that such a thing was rather beneath him) to go on the public stage with his work and get paid for it.

> *Dickens' public readings of his works — although thoroughly dependent upon his status as a writer — brought him arguably more fame and certainly more money than his original vocation.*

This appealed to him for a number of reasons. Dickens could see, first of all, that if he were successful he would make a great deal of money. Merely the American tour, for example, made him £19,000, despite the fact that he lost a fortune changing his dollars into pounds sterling. This, too, without resorting to profiteering. Dickens always disliked matinees (working people couldn't attend) and was careful to ensure that seats were available at affordable prices. It became abundantly obvious that considerably more money could have been made once the ticket touts moved in (much to Dickens' frustration) and began reselling the cheaper seats at a true 'market' rate.

We must remember, as well, that Dickens wanted to be a professional actor and, when that didn't come off, he ran a number of highly polished amateur productions in the 1840s and 1850s. This fed his appetite for acclaim without ever appeasing it. 'There's nothing in the world equal to seeing the house rise at you,

A watercolour of a Dickens reading in full flow, by Alfred Bryan.
Probably inspired by a famous Harry Furniss illustration rather
than taken from life. (The Percy Fitzgerald collection, with the
permission of the Guildhall Museum)

one sea of delightful faces, one hurrah of applause,' he had said in those days.

The public readings were also a way for the writer to reach out to his audience, and a way of encouraging them to reach back to him. Where novel writing was a solitary and drawn-out process, and its rewards delayed, readings had a kind of immediacy that Dickens must have found addictive. It is surely no coincidence either that he began his paid readings at almost exactly the time he separated from Catherine. At a crossroads, feeling betrayed and exposed, and making a fool of himself in the papers, he needed reassurance desperately. The readings gave him a chance to re-engage with and re-vivify the most enduring love affair of his life: with his public.

• WHAT WERE THE READINGS LIKE? •

Dickens designed a stage set that he took with him on tour. It included a carpet, desk, screens and a structure to support a series of gas jets that threw their light directly onto his face. He began by using a paper knife as a prop but soon abandoned this and the desk was used for practical items such as a flask of water, a handkerchief and the 'prompt copy' of the work. The whole enterprise was, indeed, 'professional'. Dickens toured with a team around him and everything was rigorously prepared. Performing was work and when touring he did not accept offers of hospitality. By the standards of the day, his 'acting' was restrained and he seems to have aimed at an intimate feel, despite the huge size of some of the auditoria. He did, however, impersonate his characters in ways people long remembered, using his body and his voice to bring them alive. He always began simply, with no portentous introduction or warm up, and ended just as soberly with no curtain calls. It would be a long evening, with an interval usually separating readings from the more serious and from the lighter areas of his work. His tours settled down to about four shows a week.

What did he read? Of course, much of his work was so lengthy that some considerable expertise in selecting and editing was required to ensure that the resulting performance was coherent. Even the short book, *A Christmas Carol*, needed work before it was suitable. Over the years, he developed readings from the longer works that were built around a central episode or theme within the narrative. So there was the trial from *The Pickwick Papers*; the life of Paul Dombey; *David Copperfield*, following the story of Steerforth and Emily and finishing with Steerforth's death in the storm; and Nicholas Nickleby at Dotheboys Hall. There were others too, especially from the later Christmas stories (some of which may have been written with readings in mind). Conspicuous by its absence was any example of Dickens' more political writing, despite the private success of *The Chimes*.

This all took its toll. Dickens put everything into his performances and they were exhausting. His American tour of 1867–68 in particular – nearly five months of gruelling work in sometimes difficult conditions – must have had a lasting effect upon his health. And yet, once he was home again, within a few months he was beginning another UK tour, this time a 'farewell' series. He devised a hair-raising new reading about the murder of Nancy in *Oliver Twist*, which by all accounts was extraordinarily powerful, but which was also a factor in his doctors stepping in to cancel the tour shortly after it had begun. There was a short series in London in 1870, but after that there were no more readings. Dickens had less than three months to live.

· 13 ·

NOT AN END

WE ALL TEND TO assume that the work of our favourite artists will endure. That, for instance, it will always
be around to inspire future generations of readers. So
it is a little sobering to return to William Hughes and
the preface to his *A Week's Tramp*. He wants to end this
personal address to his reader with a great flourish in
which he asserts the enduring qualities of Dickens'
fiction. He elevates Dickens to the membership of
what he calls 'our great English trilogy' of writers
(one assumes he meant 'English-language trilogy').
'So long as readers continue to be,' he claims, so will
they 'continue to be read'. Shakespeare is there, of
course, but who is the third? Sir Walter Scott.

Now Dickens himself (putting aside modesty) would
certainly have endorsed this (indeed, he would have
assumed that the other two names spoke for themselves),

and he would have been delighted to have been in such company. But the subsequent fate of Scott and his decline in popularity should make us wary of any assessment of Dickens' achievement that characterises it as in some way imperishable. Where Shakespeare and Dickens seem embedded in our national life, a living part of our culture, Scott (if people have heard of him) seems part of what has gone. If Dickens does seem in some way contemporary, this is down to us, the readers, and our work in keeping him fresh. It is also, of course, about the structures of power within culture, who does the reading and whose reading counts. But numbers are important.

Shakespeare is more obviously remade for successive audiences – in modern dress, as ballet, as a promenade, in the open air and so on – because his dramatic work exists as the raw material for an event before an audience. We are used to each production being different, adding a little bit more to our idea of Shakespeare. But Dickens grows too. Although we are so attached to his unparalleled depictions of the grain, the grit, the tedium and strangeness of a life that seems irretrievably buried in its historical moment, because that moment has gone, every time we understand it we make something new. Dickens changes. And, of course, his work will never come to an end. We're not done with it yet, are we?

· PLACES TO VISIT ·

THE CHARLES DICKENS MUSEUM

48 Doughty Street
London WC1N 2LX
020 7405 2127
www.dickensmuseum.com

The house in which Dickens and his family lived from
1837–39.

CHARLES DICKENS' BIRTHPLACE MUSEUM

393 Old Commercial Road
Portsmouth PO1 4QL
023 9282 7261
www.charlesdickensbirthplace.co.uk

THE GUILDHALL MUSEUM

High Street
Rochester ME1 1PY
01634 332680
www.guildhallmuseumrochester.co.uk

Permanent displays relating to Dickens' links with the
Medway towns.

ST MARY'S CHURCH, HIGHAM

The Churches Conservation Trust
Society Building, 8 All Saints Street
London N1 9RL
0845 303 2760
www.visitchurches.org.uk

ST JAMES'S CHURCH, COOLING

The Churches Conservation Trust
Society Building, 8 All Saints Street
London N1 9RL
0845 303 2760
www.visitchurches.org.uk

Two Kent churches known by Dickens and used as inspiration for his work. Both buildings are retired and are cared for by the Churches Conservation Trust. They are almost always open. Further details online.

· FURTHER READING ·

· DICKENS ·

NOVELS

Cheap, dear, hard, soft – it is just a case of picking your edition really. A tip: a quick internet search will reveal cheap second-hand editions of top-quality hardbacks like the Oxford Illustrated series.

ESSAYS

Some of the best are collected for us in the *Uncommercial Traveller*. Try, to begin with:

- 'Dullborough Town'
- 'Travelling Abroad'
- 'Night Walks'

- 'Nurse's Stories'
- 'Some Recollections of Mortality'

There is also *Reprinted Pieces*, which includes 'Our English Watering Place' (Broadstairs) and 'Our French Watering Place' (Boulogne).

To get a feel for the format in which these essays first appeared, go to Dickens Journals Online (www. djo.org.uk), which contains complete online editions of *Household Words* and *All The Year Round*.

• OTHER WRITERS •

Slater, Michael, *Charles Dickens* (Yale University Press, 2011)

Tomalin, Claire, *Charles Dickens: A Life* (Penguin, 2012)

Schlicke, Paul (ed.), *The Oxford Companion to Charles Dickens: Anniversary Edition* (Oxford University Press, 2011)

Werner, Alex and Williams, Tony, *Dickens's Victorian London* (Ebury Press, 2012)

Tomalin, Claire, *The Invisible Woman: the story of Nelly Ternan and Charles Dickens* (new edition, Penguin, 2012)

Orwell, George, 'Charles Dickens', collected in *Shooting an Elephant* (Penguin, 2003)

Also available in this series:

"How often have I said
to you that when you
have eliminated the
impossible, whatever
remains, however
improbable, must be the
truth?" *The Sign of Four*

THE
Sherlock Holmes
MISCELLANY

ROGER JOHNSON
& JEAN UPTON

FOREWORD BY GYLES BRANDRETH

978 0 7524 7152 5

Also available in this series:

"If anyone writes about
my life in the future,
I'd rather they got the
facts right." *Agatha Christie*

THE

Agatha Christie

MISCELLANY

CATHY COOK

978 0 7524 7960 6

Visit our website and discover thousands of
other History Press books.

www.thehistorypress.co.uk

12-14